$\mathcal{A}$ Lucky Day

CARLOS J. SERVER

Translated from the Spanish by Annie Crawford

www.carlosjserver.com

For you, because I owe everything to you.

For you, because you deserve everything.

AUTHOR'S NOTE

All characters and situations appearing in this book are the fruit of a playful mind. Any resemblance to reality is entirely coincidental.

If any of my readers think they see themselves reflected in a certain character, or if that character reminds them of someone they know, it just goes to show that as humans, we all have a lot in common.

"Luck is an arrow that finds its target in the least expected place."

KONRAD ADENAUER

1

August 24

There is a time of day that unmistakably defines summer: the hours between lunch and five o'clock in the afternoon. The heat is unbearable; people take refuge in the shade, leaving the streets deserted while they wait for the inferno outside to subside so they can go out once again and resume their lives. The air is somnolent; no breeze stirs the leaves, and even the birds seem unwilling to break the silence. Only the most peculiar creatures dare to brave this moment, the precise time at which our story begins.

"Jeanette, I've told you a hundred times already that you're reading the map backwards!" Adrien exclaimed as he ran a hand over his perspiring forehead. "We should have turned off six miles ago!"

"It's your fault for not wanting to ask at the gas station," his wife answered as she turned around in her seat to look at Charlie, who was stretched out asleep on the back seat of the rented Corolla.

As she contemplated him, scenes from her own childhood flashed through her mind. She remembered the trips she'd taken with her parents in their old orange Mini, during which she would always fall asleep in the back seat. Even with her legs fully extended, her feet didn't touch the other door, something that had been very comforting to her. She still recalled the sadness that had flooded through her years later when she found for the first time that she could no longer stretch out on the back seat: she'd grown older.

Jeanette had always envied the way children could fall asleep no matter where they were. Later, she thought, when we grow up, people fall into two categories: the ones who can still fall asleep in any situation, as if nothing disturbs them—and those who are incapable of sleeping unless the room they're in is completely dark, silent, and exactly seventy degrees. The thought that she belonged to the second group caused her to feel a certain regret.

With this thought, she faced forward again. It was four thirty in the afternoon on a sultry August twenty-fourth. Though Adrien had been refusing to recognize it for some time now—and Jeanette hadn't wanted to reproach him for it—the fact was they were lost, after having spent the morning at a quaint little beach on the French Riviera. It had been a little too quaint for Jeanette, who was a dyed-in-the-wool urbanite. Right now, the fact that they hadn't had any cell phone coverage for the last five minutes was beginning to fray her nerves.

"Look, there's a sign that says Sainte Marie d'Azur. The turnoff is less than a mile," she pointed out. "Why don't we stop and ask how to get back to the highway?"

"No, I prefer to continue," Adrien said. "I'm sure we'll find it up ahead."

"You heard me! We're getting off here and that's final!" Jeanette said, raising her voice and causing Charlie to stir in his sleep on the back seat. She added, effectively putting an end to further discussion, "Besides, I have to go to the bathroom."

Though Adrien knew most people thought arguing was bad for your health, he'd always considered a good argument a great way to pass the time when there was nothing else to talk about. After all, they always made up afterwards, he thought. On the other hand, he was so hot that he would actually love to stop for a while. Jeanette hadn't let him turn on the air conditioning because she said it gave her a headache.

Passing a sign announcing Sainte Marie d'Azur, they entered a village that seemed unnervingly deserted. They drove along a long street lined with houses, none more than two stories high, painted in an array of colors. On the sidewalk in front of each house sat chairs of differing sizes and shapes. All the doors had gray or green rolling blinds, pulled all the way down. The shuttered windows and complete absence of people gave the village an abandoned feel, like those towns that end up submerged at the bottom of reservoirs, eternally frozen in time.

"Everything's closed here," said Adrien, a note of reproach in his voice.

"Keep going. There's sure to be a café open somewhere downtown," Jeanette said, annoyed.

"I doubt if this place has a downtown. If we're lucky it might have a priest with a church," Adrien responded, trying to defuse the tension between them. Naturally, it didn't work.

They continued along the narrow street until they reached a small square with a few trees. Next to the square was a church, its large double doors open. Adrien and Jeanette looked at each other and nodded, agreeing that it would be best to go in and ask.

"Charlie, wake up," his mother whispered in his ear. "We're going to get out of the car for a moment."

The little boy stretched and they climbed out of the car. Adrien locked it and they walked toward the doors of the church. Peering inside, they could barely see anything; after the bright light outside, the interior was as dark as a cave. An odd but not unpleasant smell of old dust mixed with incense met their nostrils. As their eyes adjusted little by little to the low light, they were able to make out a figure at the altar with its back to them.

Jeanette asked, "Excuse me, could you help us?"

2

August 24

Julien had rung the bell twice now. Just as he was poised to leave he heard someone inside say, "I'm coming! Just a moment, please!"

He had to admit it was the most charming house in the village. The front yard was full of rose bushes that were perpetually in bloom, the white of the picket fence was always pristine—as if it had been painted only the day before—and the decorative stones were artfully arranged along the walk leading to the front door, also white. The only thing that appalled Julien was the strange obsession the inhabitants had with garden gnomes, in every possible shape and color. There was even one posed as if it were urinating. Julien had heard that if you connected the hose, water sprayed out like a sort of fountain. What kind of people wanted a dwarf peeing in their front garden? This was the question that bothered Julien whenever he had to go by the baker's house to deliver their mail.

At that moment, the door opened, revealing Bernadette, clad in a pink bathrobe, her hair wrapped in a towel. The wife of Dominique, the baker, Bernadette was a bit peculiar.

Despite the fact that she was over forty and the years had left their mark on her face, she had managed to conserve a certain youthful air. This was helped, of course, by the jaw-dropping rack she possessed, which the two children she'd borne had only improved. Apparently she hadn't been able to breastfeed and everyone in the village knew it, but for some strange reason, as if it made her a bad mother, she had always attempted to disguise it in an odd way. Whenever people were around, she would pull out her breast and pretend to give it to one or the other of the children. Predictably, the little ones ended up falling asleep on those natural pillows and everyone looked the other way as if it were nothing.

But the most notable thing about Bernadette was that she could not stop talking. She was capable of running on about trivial subjects for hours, contributing nothing new to the conversation, while simultaneously skipping from topic to topic without finishing her previous sentence. There was no doubt she was possessed of an astonishing ability that merited further study some day.

"Good morning, Bernadette! I've brought your mail," said the mailman a bit nervously, smiling from ear to ear.

"Forgive me for making you wait, Julien," Bernadette answered. "I was in the shower. I always take advantage of this time to relax, right after Dominique drops the kids off at school and goes back to the bakery."

"Don't mention it. I was admiring your yard. Especially the gnomes. I think they add such a special touch," the mailman said untruthfully but kindly.

"Really? I'm so glad to hear that someone shares my fondness for garden gnomes," said Bernadette. "My husband says I'm crazy. He doesn't realize all the best houses have them. There are lots of articles about it in my women's magazines. But of course, what can you expect from a baker?

The only thing he's read in years are cake recipes. I should have married a man of the world who would have taken me to see places like the ones you only see in good movies. Like the one that was on TV yesterday, did you see it? That one with Gregory Peck and Audrey Hepburn? Where they meet in Rome, and of course fall in love at the end. Rome! Now there's a city for you!"

Putting on his best smile, Julien pretended to listen to the interminable cascade of incoherent phrases while privately musing that if it weren't for that rack there was no way he would be here enduring the waterfall of words. He knew perfectly well that Dominique was always working at the bakery at that hour and that he would find Bernadette alone. Also, they had such a sweet little mailbox on their white fence. Seeing that admirable oval receptacle always cheered him on his morning rounds and made his work lighter. People in our village will be happier if the mailman is in a good mood, Julien thought. And of course, who was he to oppose a general increase in happiness among his neighbors? It would be unacceptable if on his account the townspeople became even more depressed than they already were after what had happened.

"By the way, Julien, is there any more news about the EuroMillions winner?" Bernadette asked.

"Not yet, I don't think. I have to go by Pierre's bar later to drop off some letters and I'll see if they know anything more. I'll let you know this afternoon," Julien answered, internally rejoicing at the excuse this gave him to return. "I'm afraid I must leave you now, Bernadette. I've got to keep doing my rounds. Have a good day."

"You have a good day too and drive carefully," Bernadette answered, giving him a big smile.

"Don't worry, I've got it under control. See you later,"

Julien said as he pedaled off on his official postal-service bicycle.

Bernadette stood looking after him from the doorway. Feeling a sudden chill, she remembered she'd been in the middle of a shower and hastened inside, closing the white door of her charming home behind her.

3

August 24

"What? Again?" M. François exclaimed indignantly to his wife Mme. Léonore. "The woman is incredible! I don't believe it. Every day she manages to surprise me more!"

"What would you like me to do, François? At least she's not robbing us. I'll speak to Paulette again tomorrow," Mme. Léonore answered. "But I warn you, I've already explained it to her several times."

Paulette, the woman who kept house for the Lefebvres, was a very good person, not necessarily a good recommendation for working as a maid, but apparently a very useful one for keeping her job no matter how incompetent she was. The basic problem was that Paulette, who came from a poor family, couldn't get used to the down comforters that you slipped into a duvet cover and that were all the rage currently. Mme. Léonore had explained to her how to make the bed several times, but Paulette's limited understanding did not extend beyond the traditional sheet, blanket, and bedspread. Each morning she made the bed in the oddest ways imaginable. One day she would use the duvet cover as a sheet, placing the naked down comforter on top of it. The next morning, after having been corrected, she would reverse the previous day's positions, putting the comforter on first, followed by the duvet cover. On other occasions she judged it best to add a sheet from another set as a top cover. The problem was that every night M. François was compelled to unmake and remake the bed. That wasn't the worst of it, though; whenever he reminded his wife that Paulette was a disaster, Mme. Léonore defended her, declaring that the maid was a very good person. This was what drove M. François up the wall. He was from the old school and it was clear to him that what had value had value and what didn't should be tossed out. He adhered strictly to this principle in all cases— except, of course, Paulette's.

M. François was the mayor of Sainte Marie d'Azur. He had occupied this post for thirty years and had belonged to five different political parties. As he put it, "What matters in a town is not the parties, but the people," and to prove it, he'd been re-elected seven times in a row by an absolute majority. At this particular moment, in addition to his job as mayor, he was president and secretary general of the Citizens of Sainte Marie d'Azur. Previously, he'd been a member of the Union for French Democracy, the Socialist Party, the Union for a Popular Movement, and the coalition Alternative for Sainte Marie d'Azur. The rigid authoritarian nature of his character dictated that any difference of opinion with his current political affiliation lead to the abandonment of that party. More simply put, if his orders were not obeyed, he left the party and founded a different one.

Basically, he was a good mayor for the village. He'd brought the music school and the health center to Sainte Marie d'Azur as well as potable water, a daycare facility, and many other advantages much appreciated by the inhabitants. His only regret was having convinced the president of the Provence-Alpes-Côte d'Azur region to establish a lottery office in Sainte Marie d'Azur—though he still remembered the day it had been inaugurated, when all was hugs and congratulations. Previously, the townspeople had had to drive almost twenty miles to play, so when Lottery Retailer No. 1 opened at Pierre's bar in Sainte Marie d'Azur, it was quite an event. A band was hired to provide music and M. François declared a holiday throughout the municipality. What happy days those had been! No one could have imagined the misfortunes that would soon befall a village as peaceful as Sainte Marie d'Azur.

"François, I'm very worried about what's happening," Mme. Léonore said. "This morning Bastian the butcher told me that a group of people have agreed to take turns standing guard in case anyone attempts to leave town today. I'm afraid they may do something rash."

"I don't think it's anything more than simple curiosity to know who the winner is," M. François said. "But just to be on the safe side, I'll ask Sergeant Chardin to go by in case anyone's more tense than usual."

"François, don't you think it would be wise to let the Gendarmerie in Cannes know? That way they could send someone, at least for tonight," his wife said in a worried tone.

"Yes, you're right. That way we'll all feel calmer," answered the mayor sadly. He sighed. "What I most wish is for tonight to be over and for everything to go back to the way it used to be."

M. François knew it was going to be difficult for things to return to their former state. The incident had been bruising for Sainte Marie d'Azur, and wounds like that were difficult to heal. How an event that was so important for their village could have gotten so out of hand was the question that had plagued M. François every single day since that terrible, fateful Friday.

"Maybe the time has come for me to step aside and allow the younger people to take over," M. François said in a contrite tone as he began to unmake the bed so he could remake it properly.

"François, none of this is your fault; these things happen," his wife said encouragingly, taking his hand with the tenderness born only of true love. "Come, let me help you make the bed. It's true Paulette seems to outdo herself with each passing day."

"What would I do without you, my love?" M. François fondly caressed his wife's cheek. By the warm light of the small bedside lamps the two proceeded to make the bed together as they did every night.

4

August 24

Jeanette walked quickly down the narrow aisle between the rows of old pews. They were dark in color, like the rest of the nave. During what was known as the Great Fear, at the start of the French revolution, invaders had set fire to the Sainte Marie church. This explained the blackish color of the stone walls inside the building that made the interior gloom even darker. Originally, the dome had boasted two levels of exquisite stained glass windows, the lower measuring more than seven feet and the upper almost three and a half. These windows had also been destroyed in the fire and bricked up during Napoleon's time for lack of resources. Three of the four towers originally constructed in the seventeenth century were knocked down to build barricades. Only the bell tower had been preserved. There were two reasons for this. The first was that few people in the village owned a timepiece, and the clock in the bell tower was the only way to tell time. Knowing the hour really wasn't essential during those times, however, since distractions were few. It was the bells that had provided a much more valuable service for the villagers of Sainte Marie, and this was the second reason the tower had been left standing. The ringing allowed those who were away from their homes working in the fields or watching over their flocks to know when they could stop work and return home for a hot meal.

At the altar, just in front of an enormous illuminated cross that hung from the ceiling, Jeanette halted before a priest who watched her in silence. Hearing a voice at the door asking for help, Father André had turned around, startled, and followed her movements. Now she was standing in front of him. Few people had entered this, the only church in Sainte Marie, in recent days. Father André had been the parish priest for almost thirty years: time enough to become well acquainted with his parishioners and to have seen it all. Even so, the situation in which the village found itself now topped everything that had come before. What most upset him was having been unaware of the seriousness of the affair until it had been too late. Now only a miracle could resolve the resulting imbroglio.

The priest welcomed Jeanette with a smile. "Good afternoon, my child. How may I help you?"

"Good afternoon, Father," responded Jeanette. "You see, we got lost looking for the highway. We saw there was a village nearby, and we thought maybe someone could tell us the best way to get to Cannes. We were thinking of stopping somewhere for a coffee and then going on. The thing is—"

"You didn't find anyone," Father André interrupted her.

"Exactly, Father. It seemed a little strange. We decided to stop at the church to see if someone could help us."

"Lately this village hasn't been what it was," Father André said. "Too many things have happened. But don't concern yourself, child. I can explain to you how to get back to the highway—and if you'll allow me, I'd be happy to furnish that coffee you were looking for."

"Please, don't trouble yourself. Telling us how to find the highway is favor enough," Jeanette answered. "We don't want to keep you. I'm sure you're very busy."

"It's no trouble. I insist. Besides, I wouldn't mind the company. I haven't had much lately," replied the priest, glimpsing an opportunity to tell an outsider about the trials of Sainte Marie.

"No, truly, it's not necessary," said Jeanette, trying to worm her way out of the invitation. The last thing they needed was to waste the whole afternoon listening to some village priest's stories, she thought, congratulating herself on the quickness of her response.

Then she heard Adrien's voice from the door. "I'll take you up on that coffee! It would help to clear my head after so much driving—if it's really no bother, of course."

The only thing keeping Jeanette from strangling her husband at that precise instant was her suspicion that the priest might not have approved of such a thing on holy ground. Father André's words brought her back to disheartening reality as she was imagining herself snuffing out the lit candles stamped with the image of St. John on Adrien's chest.

"It's settled, then! Shall we go to the inner courtyard of the sacristy? It's shaded most pleasantly, and if we're lucky we might even get a breeze," the priest said with enthusiasm. He closed the door of the church behind them and led them to the patio. It was a radical change, the somber atmosphere of the nave giving way to the courtyard's profusion of light and color. Full of roses and geraniums of every hue, it was like being in an English country garden. A majestic mulberry cast its shade over a third of the courtyard, banishing the suffocating heat. Purple stains from fallen mulberries dotted the sandy ground. Around the trunk, which measured more than three-and-a-half feet in diameter, two rows of flowerpots were arranged, each of a different color and size. Geraniums, petunias, hydrangeas, and other flowering plants bloomed from the pots, giving the impression of harmony in disorganization. Next to the flowerpots stood a table made from a heavy slab of white marble atop iron legs.

The most notable thing in the patio, though, were the two easels that stood opposite the mulberry, each with a painting propped on it. One was a typical still life of a table holding a basket of fruit, a pitcher of water, and a glass. The other was much more striking, not because of its subject, but rather, that such a subject should be found in that location. It depicted a nude woman caught in the act of bringing to her mouth the peach she held in her left hand. As soon as they entered the courtyard, Father André hastened to turn "Venus with a Peach" around, but not before Jeanette and Adrien had clearly seen what the canvas contained.

"It's a little hobby of mine," the priest said, his voice tinged with nervous embarrassment and his cheeks reddening. "The truth is I don't devote as much time to it as I'd like—my parish duties keep me too busy. Please, make yourselves at home while I prepare the coffee. It will just take a moment," he said over his shoulder as he left the patio.

"You'll 'take him up on that coffee'?? What were you thinking?" Jeanette hissed at Adrien, her face stormy. "You and I are going to have a talk when we get to the hotel. Fabulous day you're giving me, I must say. First you get us lost and now this coffee business. Besides, did you see that painting before he turned it around? He's probably a pervert or something."

"What are you talking about?" Adrien whispered back. "Can't you see he's just a typical small-town priest who's been here his whole life? If he were some kind of psychopath don't you think somebody would have noticed by now and kicked him out?"

"But didn't *you* notice there's nobody living in this town? He probably murdered them all," Jeanette said, adding in a calmer tone, "Just leave Charlie sleeping on that deck chair. An earthquake probably wouldn't be enough to wake him with all the racing around he did at the beach."

At that moment the priest reappeared, bearing a tray with a coffeepot and cups. He poured their coffee and passed the sugar. "So tell me, what brings you to these parts? I'm imagining you're on vacation, since if you lived somewhere on the French Riviera, you would already know how to get home," Father André said. "Where are you from?"

"I'm from a small town in Normandy and my wife is from Bordeaux, but we've lived in Paris ever since we met in medical school," Adrien volunteered. "I'm a traumatologist and Jeanette's a pediatrician. We were married six years ago, and Charlie was born soon after."

"That's wonderful," the priest said.

"Forgive my asking," Jeanette put in, "but is this village always as deserted as it seems today?"

"Oh, my child, if I told you . . ." the priest said sadly. "You might not believe me, but only three months ago, this was a very cheerful village."

A Lucky Day

5

May 25

Sergeant Chardin couldn't recall ever having been under so much stress. Even when the daycare center was inaugurated there hadn't been this many media interviews in the village. The week before had been fairly quiet, and the police officer had been looking forward impatiently to Saturday morning when he could indulge his secret hobby: butterfly collecting. Armed with a net for catching the beautiful creatures and attired in color-coordinated khaki pants, shirt, and hat, he made a most impressive spectacle tiptoeing around the woods every Saturday morning like an avid little boy.

At five feet five and 265 pounds, Chardin cut an imposing figure as an officer of the law. It wasn't necessary to tell people who was in charge. In spite of his impeccable manners and natural affability, everyone in the village knew he didn't tolerate practical jokes. On one occasion he'd been having a mid-morning coffee at Pierre's bar when he was approached by Julien the mailman and Florian, the mayor's son, who was studying agronomy in Lyon. The latter was spending a week in the village with his parents, since his exams were coming up in June and he was planning to stay on in Lyon until he'd finished them. Florian was quite the joker, and considered that his status as the son of the perennially elected mayor allowed him more latitude with the municipal employees than was actually warranted.

"Good morning, Sergeant Chardin," Florian said courteously.

"Florian! Well, well," answered the officer. "What are you doing here? I thought you were in Lyon studying."

"I managed to get away for a few days—I was under a lot of stress. My exams are coming up really soon, and I won't be able to leave again until July, so I decided to take a break and come home for a week to see how my parents were doing."

"Excellent, my young champion! I wish you luck on your exams," Chardin said.

"Thank you."

"Don't mention it," Chardin said. "Would you mind keeping an eye on my cap and nightstick while I go use the facilities? Pierre's restroom is so filthy I never know where to set things down."

"Sure, Sarge, no worries. We'll take care of them," Florian answered with a big fake grin.

"Thanks boys, much obliged."

Sergeant Chardin hastened toward the toilet. The stomach cramps that tormented him punctually at ten thirty every morning were particularly savage today. *Why did I have to eat so many figs last night?* he asked himself as he disappeared behind the bar.

"Hurry, Julien!" Florian said. "Ask Pierre for some food coloring. I'm sure he's got some in his stockroom."

"But what do you want food coloring for?"

"To have some fun with the fat man! We'll put it inside the cap. You know he doesn't take it off the whole day. When he looks in the mirror tonight he'll be gobsmacked—his hair will be dyed yellow!"

"Are you crazy? Chardin may seem harmless, but when he gets riled up you'll never hear the end of it. I don't want anything to do with this scheme. I know what I'm saying. I have to get back to work anyway—I've got a lot of mail still to deliver. See you later, then." He made a hurried departure, Florian's taunts of "Chicken!" ringing in his ears.

Julien's warning did nothing to dissuade the mayor's son from his practical joke. He wasn't prepared for what came next, though. No sooner had the mailman left the bar than he met M. François.

"Good morning, Julien! Making your appointed rounds as always, I see. Good work, son!" the mayor greeted him affably before turning into the bar. There he found Florian, who had just finished carrying out his scheme. The boy had left the doctored cap on the table and was prudently trying to escape before Sergeant Chardin returned from the toilet.

"There you are, son, I was looking for you," M. François said. "Your mother wants you to go to Uncle Pamphile's house with her to pick up a couple crates of apples and carry them home for her."

"Sure, Dad, I'll go right away."

Suddenly, foiling Florian's escape attempt, Sergeant Chardin emerged from the facilities. "Good morning, Mr. Mayor," Sergeant Chardin said hastily.

"Good morning, Chardin," said M. François. "I think this is the first time I've seen you in uniform without your cap."

"Forgive me, Mr. Mayor, it was only for a moment while I was in the restroom," the officer said nervously.

"Don't worry about it, Chardin," said M. François. "I've told you many times there's no need to be so formal. This village is very small—in terms of population, I mean," he added, quickly rectifying his statement for the sake of the men leaning against the bar, openly listening to the conversation. "I'm not referring to the largesse of spirit possessed by its inhabitants, of course." There was no need to lose potential votes for the sake of giving his police sergeant a pep talk.

"I was just leaving anyway. Thank you, young man." Sergeant Chardin bent to collect his nightstick and cap from the table.

M. François stopped him. "Hold on a minute, Chardin."

"Yes, Mr. Mayor?"

"I've always wanted to try on a police officer's cap bearing the official coat of arms of Sainte Marie d'Azur," said the mayor. "Since you're always wearing it, I've never had the chance. Come, let me try it on."

"Of course, Mr. Mayor. At your service," answered Chardin.

Florian realized a storm was brewing. *How could such a perfect plan have gone so wrong?* thought the future agronomist.

"*Voilà!* It fits me well, doesn't it? The important part is the perch it's hung on, Chardin," said the mayor in a voice loud enough that everyone in the bar turned to look at him. "What a good officer your father would have made, Florian!"

"Excellent, Mr. Mayor! It fits you like a glove," Chardin said, the oddness of the situation putting him even more on edge, if that were possible. He wasn't accustomed to acts of anarchy like the one that had just taken place.

M. François took off the cap and the sky began to fill with black thunderheads. A yellow ring two fingers thick encircled his head, made even more vivid by the contrast with his black, gelled hair. It almost looked as though he had a gold-foil crown on his head. All the spectators were struck dumb.

At that moment, Bastian the butcher entered the bar and stood stock-still staring at the mayor for at least three seconds. "For God's sake, François! Doesn't it seem a little early to you to be rehearsing your role in the Nativity play?" he sputtered through his laughter.

The bar exploded in hilarity. Florian didn't know where to hide himself and Sergeant Chardin couldn't figure out what had happened. M. François, anxious as always to avoid losing votes, joined in the merriment without the slightest idea of what he was laughing at. The mayor's ignorance did not go unnoticed by the clientele of the bar. They laughed even harder, which incited poor M. François to do the same.

"Mayor! Haven't you seen what you've got on your head?" Bastian finally gasped out between guffaws.

The mayor looked at his reflection in one of the bar windows and his face reddened with anger. "Chardin! I want you in my office! This minute!" he shouted, striding out of the bar. Inside, all the onlookers continued to laugh. All except two, that is.

Sergeant Chardin suddenly realized what had happened as well as what awaited him in the mayor's office. He fixed his gaze on Florian, his pupils dilated and his eyes becoming more bloodshot by the second. The natural rosiness of his cheeks spread to the rest of his face and deepened to a ripe purple hue. He resembled a coffeepot ready to explode.

Florian thought if there had ever been an appropriate moment for the earth to open and swallow him up, this was it.

The general laughter filling the bar suddenly died, as the patrons began to fear the worst.

"I'll kill you!" Chardin shouted. "I swear I'll kill you! No, better I'll kill myself. Or first I'll kill you, and then myself." The salient point seemed to be that someone had to die. Florian, in a fine display of loquacity, stuttered, "I didn't, um . . . I mean . . . no . . ."

Snatching up the offending cap, Sergeant Chardin left Pierre's bar, preparing himself to receive what would no doubt be the worst tongue-lashing of his life.

In reality, the affair didn't come to much. Sergeant Chardin was put on night shift for a couple of months and Florian decided he had a lot of studying to do and left for Lyon that same afternoon. M. François's wife came to his rescue with the judicious application of a good dye. The main lesson taken away by the onlookers was that it wasn't a good idea to joke around too much with the rotund sergeant, and the topic of the cap was studiously avoided from that day forward.

The truth was that even without taking the events of that fateful day into account, the huge number of vehicles and people that had gathered that Saturday in the village was beginning to try Sergeant Chardin's patience. In fact, if two of his men hadn't been out sick, leaving only himself and one other officer on patrol that morning, he would gladly have gone butterfly-hunting in spite of the one-of-a-kind spectacle taking place in Sainte Marie. What intrigued the sergeant most was how many women had gone to Mary's Beauty Salon that morning. Apparently the ladies of the village thought that the chance of appearing on television merited going all out to look their best.

Directly in front of the sergeant was a TV camera set up to record the newsworthy event. Dressed in a white pantsuit, a thirty-ish newscaster with short blonde hair and green eyes was having her already excessive makeup retouched prior to going on the air. The makeup artist finished, the cameraman gave the signal, and she began to speak. "We're in Sainte Marie d'Azur, a peaceful village of only seven hundred souls located in the heart of the French Riviera. Today more than two hundred journalists of thirty different nationalities have converged on this spot to cover what is doubtless the news story of the year. Yesterday, one of Sainte Marie D'Azur's seven hundred twelve inhabitants became a multimillionaire overnight thanks to winning the largest prize offered by any lottery in the world: 152 million euros. The lucky winner of the EuroMillions lottery was the only player to get all eight numbers right on a ticket bought last Saturday at the lottery retailer, also the village bar. So far, the identity of the lucky winner remains unknown, in spite of all the media gathered here today. All of us are impatiently waiting for that person to make an appearance in the lottery office with the winning ticket that officially designates him—or her—as the luckiest person in the world. There can be no doubt that this is a red-letter day for Sainte Marie d'Azur, which, thanks to the prize money, will soon become the happiest village in France."

"Cut! Perfect," said the cameraman. "Now what?"

"Now we wait for him to show up," the blond reporter said, as the artist retouched her makeup again.

A Lucky Day

6

August 24

"May I serve you a little more coffee?" Father André asked Jeanette, moving the delicate porcelain pot toward her.

"Thank you, you're very kind," she answered politely.

As Jeanette spooned sugar into her coffee, a light breeze blew across the patio from the sacristy, lifting the straight black hair Adrien loved so much. In fact, Jeanette's hair had driven him wild from the moment they'd met in medical school. He loved the color, the shine, but above all, the marvelous fragrance that wafted from it. It reminded him of all the beautiful moments they'd experienced together. The aroma her hair gave off continually bewitched him. She, of course, knew this, but enjoyed asking him what he was doing just to hear him say how wonderful her hair smelled.

Though the sun beat down mercilessly on the half of the patio not shaded by the immense mulberry, the temperature underneath its branches was perfect. The tranquility of the moment was a stark contrast to the state of unease that had pervaded the village during the last few months.

"I recall having read something about it on the Internet

some time ago," Adrien said. "Naturally it must have been a hugely important event for the townspeople."

"Imagine winning a prize like that," Jeanette said with a sigh. "What happened to the lucky winner? I imagine he must have lots of friends now," she added ironically.

"The truth is it would have been better for everyone if that prize had never been won by someone from the village," Father André cut in somberly.

"Why do you say that? It must have brought a lot of wealth to the community," said Adrien.

"All it brought was misfortune," continued Father André. "The day after the winning numbers were announced, the whole village turned out to celebrate. You can't even imagine the number of journalists that showed up to cover the event. Looky-loos from everywhere jammed the streets. Executives from banks across the French Riviera raced each other here to see if they could hook the lucky winner. Even a contingent of salesmen from various luxury-car dealerships showed up hoping to sell their latest model to 'the luckiest man in the world,' as the press had dubbed him. The mayor declared a holiday for everyone in the village and hired a band to stroll through the streets playing music all that Saturday. No doubt the happiest person of all was Pierre, who made a killing at his bar, putting tables out on the street in order to accommodate the avalanche of customers. Even I received orders from the archbishop to ring the church bells all morning. The women dressed up in their Sunday best and the husbands who didn't have to work that day paraded them around town. Pierre's bar was the most popular spot because that was where the winning ticket had been stamped. Naturally everyone thought—we *all* thought—that the lucky winner would reveal himself so we could share in his joy."

Wide-eyed, caught up in the story, Adrien and Jeanette

watched Father André.

The priest continued. "The hours went by and people began to get nervous. The mayor had to make several announcements asking people to please be patient and enjoy the moment. Nonetheless, the murmurs continued to get louder. Then the conjectures started about who the winner could be. The press wouldn't stop badgering Pierre to find out who it was, and the villagers were even more insistent. They started trying to remember who played the lottery on a regular basis and checking to see if everyone they'd thought of was present.

"Evening finally arrived, and most of the media decided to depart. The townspeople retired to their homes and the streets emptied little by little, leaving only a small group that gathered at the town hall. There the mayor told them what had happened was logical, that the winner must have been intimidated by all the uproar and was no doubt waiting for it all to die down before showing himself. After all, he or she had three months to claim the prize. We all admitted that the mayor must be right. A tiny village like ours where nothing ever happens wasn't used to this sort of upheaval and of course the amount of the prize was so astronomical that even I still don't have a clear idea of how much money 152 million euros actually is."

"Sure. It makes perfect sense," Adrien said. "If I won that much money I wouldn't even tell my own father."

"Just listen to yourself!" Jeanette scoffed. "You're incapable of keeping a secret. He can't even eat a sweet roll on the sly without fessing up." She turned to the priest with a moue that Father André found charming.

"So in the end, who turned out to be the 'luckiest man in the world'?" Adrien asked ironically.

"That's just the problem, my son," answered the priest. "No one knows."

"I'm sure the winner just decided not to say anything to anyone and went to some other town to collect the prize," said Jeanette. "No doubt wanting to avoid envy and people who would try to take advantage of him—since there are always hordes of them in cases like this," she added, to dispel any impression of crass materialism her statement might have made.

"Actually, to this day, no one has claimed the prize," said Father André, his tone very serious. "Today is the three-month anniversary of the lottery, and if the winner doesn't appear with the ticket by midnight, all the money goes back to the Ministry of Finance."

"I can't believe it!" exclaimed Jeanette. "Is it possible someone would give up that amount of money? Maybe the winner still doesn't know he won, or lost the ticket. It has to be something like that—what other reason could there be?"

"You could be right, child," affirmed the priest. "But since the lottery, many things have happened in this peaceful village that may have made the winner afraid to show his face for fear of reprisals on the part of some of his neighbors. People have spent the last three months conjecturing about one villager after another, and all it's brought those unlucky souls is misfortune. In the end we're no better off than we were at the beginning; no, truthfully, we're worse off than we were."

7

June 23

"Oh my God, Florian! You're killing me. I don't know what you're doing, but for the love of God, don't stop!"

Stephanie started to kiss his neck and give him love bites that began to irritate her lover's skin. Florian concentrated harder on not finishing too soon. He was only too aware that the pharmacist was in the full bloom of womanhood whereas he was only a young student without much experience. Of course he'd had a few exploratory adventures at the university, but this was a much more serious affair. A married woman wasn't in the same league; it wasn't even the same sport.

Florian tried to distract himself from what he was doing by thinking of unpleasant things. The most unpleasant, hands down, was what would happen if his father found out about this. He could already imagine him shouting in the living room, accusing Florian of being the black sheep of the family and the whole village. Of course his mother would be standing next to him crying and asking where she had gone wrong. Florian realized that thinking about this was working quite well.

"Rip my shirt off!"

This brought him back to the present. Stephanie kept giving sexy little cries and her face was flushed. This, taken together with her red hair and abundant freckles, made her in this moment the most beautiful woman in the world in Florian's eyes. He took a firm grip on both sides of her shirt in order to do what she had asked.

"No, wait! I'd better unbutton it instead. It was a gift from my mother."

When his arms couldn't take any more, he turned her around and backed her up against the shelving. Still in her bra and lab coat, Stephanie braced herself against the jumbo-sized packages of adult diapers.

"I can't wait any more, baby!"

"No! Wait, not yet! Hold out a little longer!"

What? I can't believe this, Florian thought. He'd been giving it to her for twelve whole minutes already. He knew it because his watch had beeped, as it did every hour on the hour, at the precise instant he'd begun, and on the wall next to the shelves in front of him there was a huge clock that read 4:12. To Florian, twelve minutes seemed more than reasonable . . . really, it was almost a record, judging by the statistics he saw in his men's magazines. Maybe those magazines weren't telling the truth? After all, he'd once read that the best cure for a hangover was to cut a lime in half and rub your armpits with the pieces. He'd done it so much one semester the hair in his pits started to turn green. It hadn't helped much with his hangovers, but he'd saved a ton of money on deodorant.

Thinking about all this had distracted him again so successfully that he saw he'd managed to hold out for fourteen minutes and forty seconds. Suddenly the rousing notes of the Marseillaise filled the room. The cell phone in the pocket of his pants on the floor was ringing.

Arise, children of the Fatherland . . .

"What the hell is that?" the pharmacist yelled between gasps.

"It's my dad's cell. I borrowed it from him," Florian panted. "Just ignore it. We're almost there."

. . . The day of glory has arrived . . .

The cell phone continued to ring as the lovers quickened their pace, panting harder and harder. Packages of diapers and bottles of vitamins fell from the shelves unnoticed.

. . . Against us stands tyranny . . .

"Is that damn phone never going to stop?!" Stephanie yelled, her jaw almost dislocated.

"I'm coming! I'm coming!" cried Florian.

"Yes! Yes!"

. . . To arms, citizens! Form your battalions!
March, march,
Let impure blood . . .

"Yeeeeeessssssss!!!!"

. . . water our furrows!

Bada-bing bada-boom, thought Florian.

They picked their clothes up off the floor of the stockroom behind the store and dressed as Florian explained that his cell phone had fallen into the sink while he was helping his mom wash dishes. Since it was ruined, his dad had lent him his so he could let Florian know when he needed to be picked up from the town hall. He was thinking about going through the stuff in their storage shed and taking all the junk they no longer had any use for to the main square to be burned in the bonfire in honor of Saint John that night.

"You were amazing," he told Stephanie, with the face of a lovesick calf.

"You were good too, but right now I need you to leave because it's almost four thirty and I have to open the pharmacy," she answered, opening the stockroom door and walking toward the registers. "I don't want people to see you leaving."

"I'm going." Florian took the phone from his pocket and clicked on the last missed call. "I'm just going to call my dad to see where I'm supposed to pick him up."

"Can't you call him from the street?" Stephanie was getting nervous. The last thing she wanted was for there to be talk in the village, and especially in this case, since it was well founded.

Florian waved a hand at her to silence her since the phone was already ringing. "Hi Dad." He listened for a second. "Sorry, I couldn't pick up in time." Another pause. "Oh. You'd been calling for a while. I don't know, maybe the ringer was turned down." He listened. "Okay, pick you up at the door in five. Bye."

He kissed the pharmacist on the lips. She opened the door and looked up and down the street. No one was in sight. Florian stepped outside and they kissed again, longer this time.

As he drew back, Florian noticed Father André, who had

just turned the corner from his church and was staring fixedly at him. Florian had parked next to Pierre's bar, which meant that unfortunately he was going to have to pass next to Father André, who hadn't moved from his spot. He set out, wondering if the priest had seen him kissing Stephanie. It would be better for him if he hadn't, since Father André would undoubtedly tell Florian's father. The images that had gone through his mind a few minutes before returned. He reached the priest.

"Good afternoon, Father André," he said, looking at the ground and praying the clergyman wouldn't say anything.

"'Good afternoon'?? That's all you have to say? 'Good afternoon'?" Florian's heart sank. "You're coming to confession this minute unless you want your father finding out what I just saw." Father André was really angry. "Aren't you ashamed? Especially considering who your father is? And with a married woman!"

Florian began to fear someone might overhear them. The good thing was that during the summer at that hour of the afternoon, people took refuge in their houses and didn't begin to come out again until at least five.

"My dad's waiting for me to pick him up right now at the town hall. If I'm late I'll have to come up with a good explanation."

The priest seemed to calm down a little. "All right. I'll let you go now, but I expect you at confession at nine o'clock tomorrow morning."

"But, Father, it's the St. John celebration tonight and I'm going to be out late!" Florian mustered up the expression of wide-eyed innocence he had found useful on other occasions. "Couldn't I go after lunch?"

Father André's voice rose. "Tomorrow morning at nine!

And make sure you're there on the dot if you don't want me to tell your father."

"Okay . . . I'll be there at nine," said the young future agronomist in a resigned tone.

Florian climbed into the car and went to pick up his father who was waiting for him under the shade trees that lined the sidewalk in front of the town hall. They spent the afternoon organizing the storage shed and loading a ton of old junk into the back of the pick-up. M. François kept asking how it was possible to accumulate so much clutter every year when they always took advantage of the St. John celebration to clear out their shed. Where did all this stuff come from? When they were finished packing up the truck, they drove to the village square where there was already a pile of old furniture. Sergeant Chardin and one of his two officers helped them unload. Since the day Florian had doctored his cap, the sergeant had not said a word to him besides hello and goodbye, and today was no exception. When all was in readiness for the celebration, the mayor and his son went home to rest and prepare for the evening.

By eleven p.m. the village square swarmed with activity. Pierre had put out a table with a beer dispenser in front of his bar and the town hall had set up several rows of tables with wooden chairs as it did every year. The tradition was for members of the community to prepare food at home and then bring it to the celebration to share with their neighbors. Housewives competed with each other to see who brought the best dish or the most novel. There was a little of everything, from roast meats, fish, salads, and vegetables to fruit and desserts of all types. The town hall provided the drinks. Later on, at midnight, the bonfire would be lit, and as it died down, people would gather and dance around the embers to the music of the Orchestra Fantaisie. This musical ensemble had provided entertainment for the St. John celebration every year since M. François had been mayor. Their music was a bit old-fashioned for the young people's taste, but everyone else loved it.

Dinner proceeded in the usual way; the men, as always, ordered drinks from Pierre's bar and sat down together to chat. At one table were Dominique, Bastian the butcher, Julien, and Armand, who owned the hardware store. Conversation was animated and centered on the soccer players who would be going to the World Cup. Joviality reigned until the subject of the players' salaries came up. One thing led to another and the talk eventually turned to the lottery prize.

"What the soccer players make is small potatoes," Armand said. "I'd rather win a prize like that. I would be richer, and besides, no one would know who I was."

"If I won it," Bastian took up the thread, "the first thing I would do would be get on a plane to Switzerland. I would open an account there and not tell a soul."

"Not even your wife?" Julien asked.

"Her least of all!"

Everyone laughed uproariously. By that time of night, they had all had a few drinks, especially Dominique, who had listened to the conversation without comment for several minutes now.

"I would continue with my normal life," Julien said, entertained by the conversation. "Then after a while I would disappear forever."

All laughed at this with the exception of Dominique, whose head was starting to spin from too many drinks. "You all think that's a great idea, huh?" he cut in, his tone stony. The laughter around the table died. "So if any of you won, you'd leave town as quickly as possible without saying a word to anyone. Listen, there was a reason that prize came to this village, and it should stay in this village," he ended emphatically.

"What are you saying, Dominique?" said Julien, trying to calm him down. "We were just joking about what we would do if we'd been the ones to win. With that much money, anyone would want to leave the village and see the world."

"Your problem is that you're a failure that no woman has ever been interested in. You think you're never going to get out of here and that's why you're so anxious to leave." Dominique was definitely starting to get disagreeable.

"That'll do, Dominique!" Bastian interrupted. "I think you've had enough to drink for tonight." He reached out to take Dominique's glass, but the baker swatted his hand away.

In a drunken stupor, Dominique staggered to his feet and almost fell. "You don't get to tell me when I've had enough! Not you, not anybody. I can take any of you down, even if I have been drinking!"

The buzz of conversation at the adjoining tables began to fade away as the townspeople went quiet and turned toward the men's table, wondering what was going on and the reason for the shouting. Bernadette hastened over to her husband when she saw him standing up and yelling.

"What's happening here, Dominique?" she asked him.

"Nothing, sweetheart." He swayed alarmingly. "These guys think Sainte Marie isn't good enough for them. They're a bunch of embittered bastards who only want to get away from the village."

"Come on, Dominique," said his wife. "It's time for us to go home."

"I think it's best, Bernadette," Armand said. "If you want, I'm parked right over there. I can take you both home."

"I would be grateful, Armand," answered the baker's wife. "I don't think I can handle the car and my husband at the same time."

"I'm not going anywhere until after the bonfire," spluttered Dominique.

"Forget it," Bernadette said. "We're leaving right now. The bonfire won't start for another hour and you're in no condition to stay."

"Shall we go? The car's parked on the street in back of the square," Armand said, standing up and rummaging in his pocket for his keys.

"I said I want to see the bonfire!" insisted Dominique.

"I can accompany you as well if you'd like," Julien said to Bernadette with a big smile.

Dominique continued to babble. "I'm watching the bonfire . . ."

"There's no need, Armand can handle it." Bernadette gave Julien a brief smile.

While the others were deciding on the best way to get Dominique home, the baker himself had one fixed idea in his head: he'd stayed for the St. John bonfire every single year of his life, and if he didn't see it this year, it would be bad luck.

Everyone stood up to help Bernadette with her husband. Dominique chose this moment to snatch up the bottle of cognac from the table and make a run for the mountain of junk piled at the other end of the square. As he ran he stuffed a paper napkin from the table into the neck of the bottle, fashioning a sort of Molotov cocktail. The men from the table lit out after him, but he had the element of surprise in his favor and was well ahead of them. When he reached the pile of wood and old furniture, Dominique ran into Sergeant Chardin.

"Out of my way, fatso!" he snapped.

Before Chardin had time to react, Dominique had lit the napkin and hurled the bottle onto the pile. The sergeant threw himself on the baker, but it was too late. The fire blazed up and quickly enveloped the mountain of junk. Stepping back instinctively as the scorching heat threatened to sear their faces, the townspeople stood watching the blaze.

As the rest of the villagers gathered around the bonfire, the Orchestra Fantaisie, believing the time had come for them to play, struck up the Sainte Marie d'Azur anthem.

This year the bonfire in honor of St. John had started an hour early.

8

August 24

"Who's next?" asked Bastian. He wore a full-length white apron. The butcher was meticulous about cleanliness and order at work and rarely dirtied himself. It seemed almost miraculous to the women of the village that after spending the whole day carving up chops and mincing meat his apron could be so pristine. The truth was that Bastian changed it more than ten times a day. He couldn't bear to have bloodstains on his clothing—it gave him the creeps.

Though he was a very good butcher who performed his duties well, his true passion was archaeology. His father had spent his life as the village butcher and hadn't done badly. The trade had afforded him a higher standard of living than most of his neighbors, and his hope was to provide for his son the education he himself been denied because of the precarious financial situation he'd grown up in. Every summer Bastian's father closed the butcher shop for three weeks, saying he had to visit family in Nord Pas de Calais, 680 miles from Sainte Marie d'Azur in the north of France. In reality, he had no relatives in Nord Pas de Calais or anywhere else, at least none he would choose to spend three weeks visiting. During the rest of the year, he spent his evenings planning elaborate trips to world capitals. When they came back to the village after their summer vacations, no one in the family would reveal where they'd been or the marvels they'd seen. At first it had been almost impossible for Bastian to resist telling his neighbors how fantastic his trips had been, especially when others enthused about their own. But after a while, when people would ask Bastian about his summer vacation, he would merely say it had been the same as usual.

The butcher had fond memories of the many places he'd traveled throughout his childhood, each trip more fabulous than the last. One summer they'd visited several cities in France before winding up their vacation in Paris, where they'd stayed four days. The first day they'd taken a tour of the Louvre, which hadn't held much interest for Bastian until they got to the ancient-art galleries. These were a revelation for young Bastian. He was so fascinated he insisted his father allow him to return every day for the rest of their stay. The art that captivated him the most was from the Assyrian empire. From that time on, it became a passion. After that trip, Bastian filled the house with books on the Assyrians and decided he would study either ancient history or archaeology.

He was always a good student though he helped his father in the butcher shop afternoons and weekends. When he finished high school and enrolled at the university, his father beamed with pride. A month before Bastian was due to leave for college, however, his father suffered a stroke. He survived, but spent three months in the hospital, and when he was released, he was unable to move the right side of his body. Bastian's parents begged him not to give up his dream of studying archaeology, but he replied that it could wait. He would take over the butcher shop for a few years and once he'd saved enough money to support them all, he would take up his studies again.

The years passed, and Bastian grew accustomed to the comfortable lifestyle his trade afforded. His butcher shop was the only one in the village and his artisanal sausages gained so much fame that people came from everywhere on weekends to buy them. He spent his evenings on the Internet and glued to his archaeology books, and when he had the time he traveled to Southeast Asia to see Assyrian ruins.

"It's my turn, Bastian," answered the mayor's wife.

"Good morning, Madame Léonore! What can I get for you?"

"Some lamb chops, please. Two pounds or so."

"Lamb chops coming up." Bastian took a rack of lamb from a hook and sliced the chops off it with the impressive speed and precision of a bank teller counting bills.

"Did M. François enjoy the steaks the other day?" he asked, his knife flashing.

"They were delicious, Bastian, but I've told my husband he can only have them once a month, otherwise his cholesterol will go sky-high," Léonore said. With a significant glance at the other customers, she added, "You've got to take care of yourself at our age."

As the customers began to discuss cholesterol, Bastian interrupted. "Ladies, the products sold in this butcher shop contain very little cholesterol. High cholesterol comes from processed food and a sedentary lifestyle. A good diet should include vegetables, legumes, fiber—and meat, of course."

"That's true," put in another customer. "I won't allow processed foods in my house, and I try to avoid fried food as well."

Bastian took up the topic, reiterating the evils of fried and processed foods, successfully dodging a potential witch-hunt against meat.

The door opened, admitting a group of approximately fifteen people, making the butcher shop suddenly very crowded. From the back, a man of forty-five or so called, "Good morning, Bastian. Do you have our order ready?"

"Madame Léonore, if you'll allow me, I'll just ring up these people's order," the butcher said courteously to the mayor's wife, giving her a big smile. "I have it ready and all bagged up. It will only take a minute," he added.

45

"Of course, don't worry about it. I'll wait." Inside, Madame Léonore wasn't quite as unperturbed as she appeared.

Bastian brought out a large number of bags, all containing the same thing, a variety of artisanal sausages. He handed a bag to each member of the group, most of whom were foreigners, and they went out one by one. When all had been served, the man who had originally addressed Bastian came to the counter and handed him an envelope.

"Done! And now, Madame Léonore, what else can I get for you besides the chops?"

"Give me some Majorcan sausages like the ones those people bought. Where did they all come from, by the way?"

"They're good customers! I have a contract with a tourist agency. On Saturdays they take a group of tourists to see the Roman ruins and then they visit Sainte Marie so the tourists can buy sausages. I prepare a bag with the same assortment for everyone. The guide pays me and the cost is included in the overall price of the tour. From here they go on to the church to see the image of St. John and then to Pierre's bar for breakfast."

"That's a good business if you get a guaranteed group every Saturday," commented one of the ladies. "Things must be going well for you."

"Oh, I scrape by," Bastian lied, as he had as a child when talking about his summer vacations. "Times are tough. Ever since that lottery business, people are buying less meat."

"It can't be because of that, Bastian," contributed another customer. "It must be the heat. In summer people like to eat lighter foods like salads or cold soups."

Once again, the butcher shop filled with conversation as customers gave each other their various summer recipes. Bastian took a deep breath; again he'd dodged a bullet. His parents' training had proved to be very useful!

9

July 1

"Dominique, we've been sitting at the table for five minutes now!" Bernadette yelled at her husband from the terrace.

"Be right there, I'm just watching the end of the sports news," her husband called from inside the house.

Bernadette took great care over all the details in her home. Her terrace was a testament to her wannabe status. An oval table of fake teak, surrounded by six chairs of the same material, occupied the place of honor in the center. Over it extended a patio umbrella not quite large enough to shade the whole table. To one side stood a small cart containing dessert plates, trays, and bottles. Plastic placemats stamped to look like rattan adorned the table, and atop them sat full place settings consisting of plates, silverware, and glasses, even in the places no one was sitting. Bernadette thought that all her valued family members deserved a place setting just in case someone showed up at a mealtime and it became necessary to invite them to stay. This had never actually happened, but she thought it might one day and she didn't want to be caught unprepared.

"Why is Daddy taking so long?" asked Noé, the younger of their children. "I'm hungry, Mommy!"

"Because Daddy's a wimp," his brother quickly answered.

His mother pinched his right arm just below the shoulder. Dominique Jr. let out a howl of pain as his mother scolded him. "Where did you learn a word like that?"

"Jeez, that hurt!" he whined. "You're always pinching me. It really hurts!" He squeezed his eyes shut for a minute. "Grandpa always says Daddy's a wimp and he's never going to amount to anything."

"What's a wimp, Mommy?" asked Noé, turning an innocent face to his mother.

"You see what you've done?" Bernadette pinched her older son again. He gave another yelp and began to rub his arm to ease the pain as his mother went on. "Noé, it means your father is a really good man who works hard so all of us can be happy," she explained, regarding him with tenderness.

"Then I want to be a wimp too when I grow up," pronounced the little boy.

Dominique Jr. and his mother burst into laughter and Noé joined in, happy that what he had just said was so important, though he wasn't quite sure what they were laughing about.

Dominique Sr. chose that moment to come out onto the terrace where he found his family laughing hysterically.

"What did I miss?" he asked with a smile.

Bernadette stopped mid-laugh and frowned. "Be quiet and sit down. You do this to us every day!"

"It's your fault! You insist on us eating on the terrace

whenever the sun's out. If you would at least let me bring out the TV so I could watch sports."

"That's all we need. To eat on the terrace and watch TV. Have you ever seen any family in a movie eating on the terrace with the TV on? This is an elegant home, and we don't watch TV during meals. We converse," his wife said.

"And what do you want us to 'converse' about?"

"I don't know. About whatever normal families talk about at mealtimes. Talk about whatever you want, just not politics or religion. Nice people don't talk about those things."

"If you want I can tell you how pissed off I am at the sports announcer. He spends ten minutes talking about Paris Saint-Germain and Olympique de Marseille and when it's time for him to talk about the other FCs he says he's running out of time. So then he crams eighteen other first-class clubs into the next two minutes along with twenty-two second-class ones, not to mention basketball, handball, track and field, Tiger Woods's master stroke in a golf tournament in God knows what Asian country, thirteen minor sports, and the human interest story of the day which is always something about how the Canadian senior women's lawn-bowling league has just won the European prize in Saint-Tropez. In this country, if you're not a fan of Olympique de Marseille or Paris Saint-Germain, you might as well buy yourself a Ouija board if you want to know how your soccer team's doing," complained Dominique self-righteously, as if his harangue had somehow made things better in the world.

"That's all I need, more talk about soccer. Can't you think of something more interesting and proper to talk about in front of our children?" Bernadette said, arching her eyebrows in the boys' direction. "We could discuss something stimulating like art or history." She looked toward her children, hoping for a reaction, but their attention was on their food and they were paying no attention to their parents' conversation.

There was silence around the table for a couple of minutes, enough time for Bernadette to imagine what her life could have been if she hadn't married the village baker. Her mind flew to exotic places like India or an island in the South Pacific, where she imagined living dangerous, romantic adventures at the side of a man who looked like the star of a Colombian soap opera. How, after protecting her from the most ruthless enemies imaginable, he would take her in his strong arms and kiss her, a long, deep kiss, after which they would make love for three days without leaving their elegant suite in a magnificent hotel.

"I've got a subject of conversation!" The voice of her elder son jarred her out of the fantasy that was beginning to send agreeable sensations through her body.

"And what would that be, Dominique? I know you . . ." his mother said warningly, fearing a resurgence of the "wimp" topic. "What you need to do is finish your lunch like your brother."

"Okay, if you don't want me to tell you, I won't. But I know who won the EuroMillions."

His parents exchanged a look before fixing their eyes on their son. How could a child have found out something the whole village had been dying to know for days?

The boy, well aware of the curiosity he had succeeded in arousing in his parents, put another bite of meat into his mouth to prolong the moment.

"Go on. Now you have to tell us!" his father insisted.

Dominique Jr. swallowed and took a sip of water, then began to explain. "My friend Patrice is an altar boy at the church, right? This morning at school he told us that on Sunday when Mass was over and everyone had left, he was clearing away the stuff when the mayor came in with Julien the mailman. They were both really nervous and they asked for Father André, saying they needed to talk to him right away. Patrice said he was in the sacristy and they told him to go get him as fast as he could. So Patrice goes to look for him, and when they come back into the church, the mayor looks at him, so Father André tells him to go wait in the sacristy. But Patrice is no dummy, so he leaves the door open a crack so he can hear what they're talking about."

Dominique's parents stared at their son, riveted by his story. Bernadette couldn't have come up with a better topic herself.

"So the mayor," young Dominique continued, "begins to tell Father André that the village is facing the biggest challenge in its history and that the results can have catastrophic consequences for Sainte Marie if the lottery problem isn't handled right. Father André asks them how he can help. The mayor tells him that the only ones that can throw any light on the situation are Julien and the priest. He says Julien knows who the winner is but denies it and refuses to tell him who it is. So the deal is Father André has to hear Julien's confession and that way he can find out who won the EuroMillions.

"So Father André gets really angry and throws his arms up in the air and says may he remind them that even if Julien tells him who it is, a priest can never reveal what's been said to him in confession. The mayor says that Father André has already told stuff he learned in confession, to him and other people from the village too. That everybody knows that when the priest has a couple of glasses of wine at the bar he always ends up gossiping about things people have told him in confession.

"At this, Father André loses it and says, all furious, that it's not the same thing and that if he's told things from confession before, they were only minor details, nothing important, and besides, it was a slip of the tongue. Patrice said that meanwhile Julien was trying to get away and insisting he didn't know anything, but the mayor had him by the arm and kept reminding him of his civic duty as a government employee. They argued for a while until Father André finally agreed to hear Julien's confession, but he warned the mayor he wouldn't tell him anything.

"So Julien and the priest go to the confessional and they're in there for a long time. Meanwhile, M. François is waiting in a pew. A couple of minutes later, two widows from the village come in and say hello to the mayor and tell him that they're there to talk to Father André about organizing some Masses for one of their dead husbands. A few minutes later, Julien and the priest come walking up behind the widows and the mayor. M. François grabs his hat with one hand and Julien with the other, says goodbye to the widows, and tells Father André he'll be back to talk to him soon."

"And that's it?" Bernadette asked, mopping the perspiration that had begun to accumulate during her son's tale from her brow. "You told us you knew who the winner was."

"Well, Patrice thought it had to be Julien. If not, why would the mayor want Father André to hear his confession? It's obvious Julien's the winner!"

Dominique Sr. had also found the end of the story disappointing. Though it was evident to him the winner couldn't be Julien, an idea began to take root in his brain. It *was* possible that Father André, who heard confession from everyone in the village, did in fact know who the lucky person was. If Dominique played his cards right, he might be able to find out who it was and see whether the person would be willing to invest in his heart-shaped sugar-cookie factory. For some time now, Dominique had been turning over in his mind the idea of producing sugar hearts, the traditional delicacy of Sainte Marie, in wholesale quantities for export to the rest of the country. The baker had been ruminating for years on the fact that the cookies were his best-selling item and would be a sure-fire success.

The family continued their lunch. Bernadette and the children chatted while Dominique sat in silence for the remainder of the meal. When his wife asked if he was feeling all right, he excused himself, claiming a slight headache. The truth was he was busy planning how to coax the coveted name from the village priest.

A Lucky Day

10

August 24

The sky was a limpid blue. No matter where he looked, Julien couldn't find a single cloud. As he cycled along the road that led to the center of town, he inhaled the aroma of the fresh, damp grass in the orchards he passed and heard the song of the birds and the cicadas in the tall pines that lined the highway. Julien had just finished delivering the mail to the houses in the country around Sainte Marie. On hot summer days like today, mail delivery to those houses was an uphill battle, and not just in the metaphorical sense. Many houses had been built in recent years on a small hill outside the village. Doubtless it was a delightful place to live—the countryside was beautiful—but for Julien and his bicycle, it was more like torture. His back was inevitably soaked with perspiration by the time he had labored to the top of the hill, where Dominique's house was, but getting to see Bernadette made the effort more than worth it. Besides, on the way down, the breeze blew across his wet back, cooling him off in the most pleasant way. For a moment he felt truly happy and thought the day couldn't be more perfect.

More than once, the Postal Service had offered to exchange his bicycle for a moped, but he had demurred, saying he didn't see the need, given how small Sainte Marie d'Azur was. The real reason was different: the idea of driving a motorcycle terrified Julien. When he was a teenager, his friends had occasionally let him try with their motorcycles, and he'd always landed on the ground as soon as he started the thing up. One time, to the delight of his companions, who hadn't been able to stop laughing, he'd managed to wedge Cyprien's motorcycle underneath his dad's car, parked only fifty feet from where he'd gotten on the infernal machine. All the girls in the village had just happened to be present on that occasion, and Julien had never been so embarrassed in his life. He'd been just a fledgling mailman then and had always had trouble relating to girls anyway. He was the late bloomer of his group, and having made such a ridiculous spectacle of himself in front of what seemed like the entire feminine sex hadn't helped. Especially because Bernadette, whom he hadn't been able to look at without feeling a tickle in his stomach, had been among them. From that day forward, he had promised himself never again to get on a motorcycle.

When he reached the village center, Julien made directly for Pierre's bar. He wanted a cool drink, but more importantly, he wanted to see if there was any news about the EuroMillions winner. Leaving his bicycle propped against the white wall of the bar, he went inside.

"Good morning, everyone," he said.

"Good morning, Julien," Pierre greeted him from behind the bar. "All done delivering the mail?"

Julien approached Father André, who was drinking a glass of wine at the bar with Bastian the butcher.

"Good morning, Father André, Bastian," said the mailman. "I just delivered the last letters. There weren't too many today."

"Good morning, my son. We're just having a little aperitif," answered Father André, whose cheeks were becoming rosy, a sure sign that the glass he held was not his first.

"What can I get for you, Julien?"

"How about a beer? I'm feeling good today. I'll keep you company."

Pierre set a draft beer in front of the mailman and refilled Bastian and Father André's glasses. The butcher had signaled to Pierre not to serve the priest again, but Pierre hadn't seen it in time. Julien and Bastian shook their heads.

"Any news on the lottery winner?" asked Julien. "Today's the last day to collect it. If the person doesn't come forward before midnight, the prize expires and all the money goes back to the Ministry of Finance."

"That may be for the best," said Father André. "That prize has brought nothing good to this town. Quite the opposite. It will be better to just get back to normal. Let the town go back to being what it was before the whole business started."

"I think the winner's already taken the ticket out of Sainte Marie and is planning to cash it in today somewhere far from here," put in Bastian.

"And if he left the village with it, why hasn't he cashed it in already? He could have done it and decided not to come back here," Pierre contributed from the other side of the bar.

"The truth is, my children, it's a mystery," sighed the priest. "People have speculated about one neighbor after another these last three months, but I have it on good authority that none of them is the winner. For example, there were people who thought the pharmacist had won. But she herself confessed to me that she knew nothing about it . . . at

57

the same time that she confessed she'd had a liaison with a young man from the village, and her a married woman."

The others looked at each other as the priest took another sip of wine. He set down his glass and added, "And don't ask me who it is, because I'm not going to tell you." No one said anything. "All right, all right, I'll tell you. It's Florian, the mayor's son."

It was clear to everyone that Father André's verbal incontinence went far beyond what was reasonable. The best part was that he never remembered what he'd said, and when the same story he'd revealed reached his ears later he was always astonished, unable to imagine how something he'd heard in the sanctity of the confessional could have gotten out. What was the world coming to, he asked himself, when no one could keep a secret any more?

"But what are you saying, Father André?!" Bastian responded, feigning surprise. "So tell me, who else in town has been sneaking around?"

Bastian knew the priest could be a gold mine when it came to this sort of rumor, and he didn't want to waste the opportunity to dig up some more dirt on his neighbors.

"Oh, my son," Father André began. "It's true this sort of thing is far from unknown in our village. Sainte Marie is a little too focused on the carnal." He hastened to clarify. "Not that I'm saying anyone is a bad person, of course." Everyone nodded in agreement. "The thing is people are on edge with this lottery business and it's easy to take a misstep."

At this point Julien stepped in and changed the subject, aware that the clergyman was well into his cups and would no doubt begin to produce incriminating evidence that would only end up causing conflict among the villagers.

"Yes, things are getting out of hand," Pierre said. "This very morning Dominique was in here talking to some other people. He's already stirred up quite a few. They're talking about organizing squads and posting them on the road leading out of town to make sure no one leaves without their knowledge."

"And what exactly do they hope to achieve by doing that?" Bastian asked scornfully.

"They think the winner will try to leave town to cash in his ticket after dark when no one's around. I think it's absurd," continued Pierre. "But Dominique maintains that the only way to restore peace in the village is for the winner to come forward. Since the prize is so large, he's sure the winner will lend money to whoever needs it. He says Sainte Marie has suffered a lot from the whole mess, after all, and the best way to make amends is for the winner to be generous with those who really need it."

"Please," snorted Bastian. "In other words, what's mine is mine and what's somebody else's belongs to everyone. What this Dominique and his henchmen want is the prize money."

"I hope they don't do anything stupid," said the mailman.

Father André's cheeks were beginning to glow like balls on a Christmas tree, becoming redder and shinier by the minute. He had attempted to follow the conversation, but the wine he'd drunk was beginning to cloud his thoughts. Not that it had been an excessive amount, but two-and-a-half glasses on an empty stomach, considering the heat of the day, was proving to be too much.

"Bastian, you know, don't you, that your wife also goes to confession quite often?" Father André interrupted. "I would almost say too often."

"What's that, Father?" Bastian said, surprised. He raised

his eyebrows, suddenly feeling the wine he'd drunk all the way down to his toes.

Julien chose that instant to collect the priest's glass. He put the clergyman's hat on his head and steered him to the door of the bar. "Come on, Father André, I'll walk you back to the sacristy. Some lunch and a nice nap will do you good."

"All right, my child, I'm coming." In his heart of hearts, Father André knew he wasn't at his best. He allowed the mailman to lead him away as Pierre watched in silence from the bar and Bastian called after him to come back and explain himself.

Julien accompanied him to the sacristy and helped him open the door. Before the mailman turned to leave, Father André looked into his eyes and said, "You're a good man, Julien, but you also need to be a brave one. I've watched you grow up in this village, and I know how you feel about Sainte Marie."

"Come, Father, that's the wine talking. Besides, it's too late now. That ship has sailed. It only lasted a couple of minutes, and it was fifteen years ago. I had my chance and I didn't take it, so someone else did instead."

"I know it's not too late," Father André said, closing the door to the sacristy.

Julien stood for a second looking at the closed door. *Now what did he mean by that?* he thought.

Not five seconds had gone by before the door opened again and the priest's flushed face peered out, his eyes almost closed. "She comes to confession too." He smiled and closed the door again.

As Julien processed what he'd just heard, a limitless happiness rose in him. Smiling from ear to ear, he ran back to the bar where he'd left his bicycle. He found Bastian and Pierre standing in the doorway.

"Julien. Did the priest explain to you what he said about my . . . ?"

But the mailman didn't stay for the rest of Bastian's sentence. He climbed onto his two-wheeled flying carpet and pedaled away, whistling.

"What happened to him?" Bastian said. "He looks like someone in the after picture of a laxative ad."

"Maybe he had to give the priest mouth-to-mouth and got drunk himself off the fumes," laughed Pierre.

"I'm serious, Pierre. Don't you think it might have something to do with my wife?" said Bastian, unsmiling.

A Lucky Day

11

July 7

Madame Babette pushed open the bakery door with her left hand and the little bell jingled as always. From her right hand dangled an enormous brown leather bag. As was her custom every Friday, Madame Babette had gone by Mary's Beauty Shop to get ready for the weekend. She'd had the same hairstyle for more than forty years. Though her natural hair color was brown, no one could remember it as anything other than platinum blond, teased up into a sort of gigantic light bulb that added almost four inches to her height. This feat of engineering would have been impossible to sustain if it hadn't been for the liters of hairspray she applied to her creation. A frequent joke at the bar was that Madame Babette's hairdo was solely responsible for the destruction of the ozone layer.

She always wore an assortment of large, colorful costume-jewelry brooches pinned to her blouse that she displayed with pride. When asked how many she owned, she always responded that she had as many as there were different types of goat cheese. There could be no doubt Madame Babette was cheerful and full of life. She'd become a widow two years earlier, and her neighbors had predicted she wouldn't outlive her husband by more than a few months, since he'd been her whole life. It was true she'd been depressed for a time, but then a friend had forced her to sign up for a tour for retired people, and they'd gone to Benidorm, Spain. From this trip, Madame Babette had returned rejuvenated, perhaps even more so than many people supposed. The village gossips said she'd met a widower on the trip and that they'd spent every minute together—both day *and* night.

"Good morning, Madame Babette," said Brigitte. She was Dominique's sister and a clerk in the bakery. "Shall I package up your usual?"

"Good morning, sweetheart. Give me the usual and add a bag of sugar hearts. I feel like splurging today," answered the widow cheerfully.

"I'm so sorry, Madame Babette! I don't know what happened today, but we're all out of sugar hearts."

"No! I was so looking forward to them. I've been thinking about them all morning."

Brigitte put on a sympathetic face. "Wait just a moment. I'm going to ask Dominique—he's baking—just in case there might be some left over in the back." She winked at the elderly lady.

"Of course I'll wait, dear," said Madame Babette.

Brigitte went into the back. The widow took advantage of her absence to check her appearance in the mirror on the wall behind the counter. Seeing that a small lock of hair was out of place, she tried to smooth it down, but the lock sprang back obstinately. Madame Babette licked her index finger and tried again to plaster it down. Faced with the combined power of hairspray and saliva, the rebellious lock relented. The widow turned away from the mirror, her satisfaction at a job well done evident on her face.

Brigitte came out at that moment with a bag of heart-shaped sugar cookies. Behind her, Dominique hustled out, taking off his floury apron. "You were lucky, Madame Babette! There was just one bag left," he said to her with a smile. "I've told you, the sugar hearts just fly out of here on Fridays, so next week make sure to get here early or you might not be so lucky. I'll say goodbye for now, I have things to do."

"Thank you, kind sir. Your sugar hearts are my favorite sweet," Madame Babette gushed. "Have a nice weekend."

Dominique picked up a large bag and rushed out of the bakery without saying goodbye. He strode through the streets of Sainte Marie d'Azur, ruminating on his plan. It couldn't fail. He'd thought of every angle, and he was sure it would work. His dream was finally about to come true.

As he passed Pierre's bar, a group of people called to him from one of the tables on the terrace.

"Dominique! Come join us! We're having a couple of beers before we go home," one of the assembled party called.

"Can't today, I've got to get home. We're going to eat soon," replied the baker without slackening his pace.

Dominique's reaction seemed odd to his friends at the bar who were in the habit of having a drink before going home for lunch, but he was soon forgotten when Pierre arrived with a tray full of beers and the talk and laughter began in earnest.

The baker turned the corner and hesitated in front of the church. For a moment he vacillated, but the rewards his plan offered were too enticing for him to turn back now. He went up to the door of the sacristy and rang the bell.

There was no response.

In his mind, Dominique's plan began to crumble. He rang again. This time the door was opened by Father André, dressed in a finely tailored cassock. The heat of the day was beginning to become oppressive.

"Good morning, Father André. I hope I'm not disturbing you."

"Shouldn't you say 'Good afternoon' instead? Seeing that it's almost time for lunch," the priest answered testily. Father André was a very progressive priest in many ways, but when it came to mealtimes, he was rather intolerant. He enjoyed the pleasures of the table and was inflexible about the hour at which his meals were served. If they were late, it put him into a foul humor, something that could only be reversed by eating.

"Yes, that's exactly why I'm here. I wanted to invite you to dine at my house, if you'd do me the honor. I know it's last-minute, but my wife and I have wanted to invite you for some time now," Dominique said.

Surprised by the invitation, Father André dithered. "Hmm . . . It's so late, I don't know." The baker had never invited him over before. "Clément was just going to make my lunch. He was going to make me grilled chicken breasts."

"Come eat with us, Father," Dominique wheedled. "Bernadette has prepared a delicious meal in your honor. Besides, I have an amazing bottle of wine, and I made an apple tart just the way you like them, with lots of apples."

"Well, I guess I could tell Clément to keep the chicken breasts for tomorrow. I wouldn't like to be discourteous to Bernadette." Father André was already mentally savoring his favorite tart while trying to imagine what exquisite dish the baker's wife might have prepared.

In reality, Dominique hadn't even told Bernadette about his intentions and hadn't the faintest idea of what she'd made for lunch. The important thing for his plan was to take the first step, which was getting the priest into his house.

"All right," said Father André finally. "Wait just a moment while I go tell Clément I won't be eating here."

He entered the sacristy and told the sacristan that he was going to the baker's house for lunch and that he would be back to prepare the seven o'clock Mass. Picking up his wide-brimmed hat, he went out into the street where Dominique awaited him.

"Ready," he said. "Where did you park?"

"Over here, Father. Follow me."

They climbed into the bakery van and drove to Dominique's house. As he pulled to the curb, Dominique began to honk the horn to let Bernadette know they were arriving. Bernadette disapproved of this custom, finding it crass, but the children loved it and always rushed out to meet their father.

The two men got out of the car and Father André lingered to chat with the children. The older boy told him how he was doing in school, while the younger grabbed his hat, put it on his own head, and ran in circles around the priest. The hat was so big on him it covered his eyes. Meanwhile, Dominique went into the house to tell his wife they had company. He found Bernadette in the kitchen leaning over the stove.

"Hello, dearest." He came up behind her and planted a kiss on her right shoulder.

"And to what do I owe this? What have you done that's

made you so affectionate all of a sudden?"

"What do you mean? Can't a man be affectionate with his own wife when he gets home?"

Bernadette crossed her arms and waited for his confession, a suspicious look on her face.

"You're right," he admitted. "I brought the priest home for lunch."

"But why would you even think of inviting someone to eat without letting me know first?! Look at the state the house is in!" Taking off her apron, she asked nervously, "Where is he?"

"He's outside with the kids. I don't know why you're getting so upset— you always put extra place settings out anyway, just in case someone shows up at the last minute." Dominique took a couple of olives from a plate on the counter.

"That's different. If a friend shows up unannounced, you invite him to join you and it doesn't matter if you don't have much to offer him. Whereas, if you expressly *invite* someone to eat, it goes without saying that you have to wine and dine him as he deserves!" Bernadette was definitely on edge. "And what am I supposed to give this man to eat? I didn't feel like cooking today so all I made was spaghetti!"

"That's it?" her husband asked incredulously. "You always make so much food we end up giving it to your parents and my sister! Well, he'll just have to make do with that. I brought an apple tart home."

"Go distract him while I figure out some kind of appetizer so we can at least give the appearance of being a decent family." She shooed her husband out of the kitchen, opened the refrigerator, and stood gazing into it with a sigh.

Once this first rough spot was over, the atmosphere became more relaxed. Bernadette prepared a nice salad with some delicious ripe tomatoes and set out dishes of cheese and almonds. They all sat down at the table and began to eat. Dominique opened a bottle of wine and filled Father André's glass. The meal progressed as usual with stories of the children and their school activities. Bernadette waited on the priest with such solicitude that his initial disappointment at seeing the platter of spaghetti faded away and he ended up thoroughly enjoying the meal.

By the dessert course, Dominique had uncorked the second bottle of wine. The effects on Bernadette were evident in the immoderate laughter with which she met each new comment. She served the apple tart, after which the kids left the table to go play, leaving the three adults alone.

"Bernadette, thank you so much for the invitation. Everything was delicious." The priest's face was as red as the tomatoes in the salad he'd eaten earlier. He'd eaten so much he was happy he'd only worn underwear beneath his cassock. Even so, the buttons were beginning to press uncomfortably against his midsection.

"Thank you, Father André. Forgive me for not having prepared something better for you, but since Dominique hadn't told me you were co—" Her husband cut her off with a sharp kick under the table. The last thing Dominique wanted was for the priest to realize he'd been lied to. All Father André knew at the moment, though, was that there was a slice of apple tart on the plate in front of him and it was exquisite.

Bernadette brought out a white china coffee set. Each cup had a flower etched on it representing a different month of the year. Father André looked at his flower, an orange blossom, and began to muse on which month it represented. The wine had clouded his brain and he wasn't thinking clearly. The coffee pot, in contrast, had an enormous tree etched on it, of some variety unknown to him.

"What a mess this whole lottery business has caused, Father, don't you agree?" Dominique couldn't wait any longer to bring up the subject.

"I do, my son." The priest dropped two lumps of sugar into his coffee. "But never fear; you'll see, it will all work out. The thing is, the winner must be a little intimidated by all the repercussions we've had," he went on. "I'm sure that before you realize it, we'll all know who it is."

Dominique was absolutely certain the priest already knew who the winner was. His plan was beginning to work. What he'd been told about the clergyman—that once he had a couple glasses of wine under his belt he was an open book about the secrets of the confessional—was true. He would have to handle the topic with delicacy, though, so that Father André didn't suspect. He didn't want the priest on the defensive.

"Go on, Father, you're so good at telling stories," the baker encouraged.

"See here, Dominique, I'm going to tell you something very interesting about this business that I'm sure will surprise you." Dominique looked at him expectantly. "The other day Julien the mailman came to confession. I don't think he knows anything about who the winner is, but he told me something even more important."

At this moment, Bernadette, who had been having trouble keeping her balance due to the amount of wine she'd drunk, lost the battle and fell over backwards.

"Goodness gracious, my child! Are you all right?" the priest asked, concerned. "You could have cracked your head open."

Dominique helped her to her feet, asking her if she was okay. Bernadette, who was a little dizzy, decided to go to her room to sleep it off, or as she put it, to rest and recover a little from the shock of her fall. Dominique led her away, leaving Father André seated at the table, drinking the last of the coffee.

What Julien had admitted to the priest in his confession of a few days prior—what Father André had been on the verge of telling the couple about—were the feelings the mailman had for Dominique's wife. Bernadette's fall had been providential because it had interrupted Father André at just the right moment.

Dominique deposited his wife on the bed and returned to finish his conversation with the priest. He had almost achieved his goal, and was impatient to hear what Father André had said was so interesting. He emerged onto the patio, smoothing his rumpled pants.

"Well, Father André, what was that you were telling me was so interesting?"

He found the priest in his chair, his head thrown back and his mouth open, emitting spectacular snores. Dominique approached him and touched his shoulder to wake him. There was no response from Father André, so Dominique shook him by the shoulder, at first lightly and then more forcefully, but it was impossible to rouse him. The good clergyman had eaten and drunk so much that even had he been in the bell tower of his church with all the bells tolling around him, it wouldn't have been enough to jar him out of his slumber. Dominique gave up. His plan had failed. When the priest woke up from his siesta, the effects of the wine would have passed, and he wouldn't reveal anything. He would have to think up another strategy. Meanwhile, at his side, Father André snored on like a rhinoceros.

12

July 10

"Once we've prepared the dough, we have to roll it out again and again, until it becomes very smooth." The muscles in Dominique's forearms tensed each time he pushed the rolling pin forward. From time to time he extended his left hand, took a couple of handfuls of flour from the large blue plastic bowl at his elbow, and sprinkled it over the dough.

Brigitte watched her brother raptly as he moved the enormous rolling pin over the dough that now almost covered the surface of the table. She could never get over how deft he was at his pastry making. Outside the bakery no one would call him overly competent with any other manual task, but once he put on his apron, he became the most skillful pastry chef imaginable.

"Once it's really smooth, you have to fold it over and over." The baker's arms flashed as he folded the dough in on itself. "This is how you get the flaky layers of puff pastry in the oven."

He slapped the dough back down on the table and began to roll it out again. Putting a hand into the blue bowl, he frowned and barked at his sister, "Brigitte, you're not paying attention! The flour's run out again."

His sister rushed to the enormous sacks on the floor that contained enough flour to keep Sainte Marie alive for a month. From the open one she took a white plastic scoop similar to a gardening trowel and ladled scoops of flour into the blue bowl until it was full. Then she tiptoed back to Dominique's side.

"I've told you a thousand times you can't run out of flour during this process," he reprimanded her in a calmer tone. "If the layers of dough stick to each other you've either got to begin again or throw the whole thing out because it'll have too much flour," he went on. "And nowadays we can't afford to be throwing anything away!"

"I'm sorry, I was just really focused on watching you and how well you do it." Brigitte knew perfectly well where to steer the conversation. As soon as his work was praised, Dominique relaxed and turned into the most docile soul imaginable.

"Well, nothing happened, after all. It's fine," he said, sitting down in a chair next to some wooden barrels. "You continue. You know what to do." Bringing his hands to his face, he rubbed his eyes.

"Okay. Now I cut a wide strip and then I cut out a bunch of triangles, all the same size." Brigitte went on working while her brother looked on from across the kitchen, fatigue evident on his face. As he watched her he thought that even another hundred years working with him in the bakery wouldn't be enough to make her any less clumsy than she was now.

Brigitte separated the triangles, sprinkled the table with flour, and arranged them next to the other triangles.

"And now I put the chocolate shavings on top and roll them up point first."

Her brother couldn't get Father André's visit the other day and how his luck had turned against him out of his mind. His head ached from trying to figure out a new way to get the name of the lottery winner out of the priest. As many times as he turned it over in his mind, he couldn't come up with a solution.

Meanwhile, at the large table in the center of the bakery, Brigitte had fashioned something that looked more like an enormous cannellone than the croissants she had been aiming for. There could be no doubt about it, thought Dominique; this woman wasn't cut out to be a pastry chef. She couldn't make bread either. The last time Dominique had caught the flu, he'd kept going to work as long as he could, but by the fourth day he hadn't even been able to get out of bed and had been forced to stay at home. Brigitte had insisted there was nothing to worry about, that she could at least make the most basic baked goods. She had told him firmly that even though there would be no tarts that day, at least the townspeople would still be able to eat their daily bread. Dominique could still hear her: *Not one day without bread in Sainte Marie!*

There had been bread that day, but the first batch had been so hard and burned it couldn't be sold. To compensate, Brigitte had put too much yeast into the second batch and the dough had expanded so much it had finally exploded all over the oven. On the third try, however, the bread had come out beautifully, and she'd sold every last loaf. Brigitte was so excited she was almost in tears, thinking about how proud her brother would be.

The cases of food poisoning had begun a couple of hours after Brigitte took the bread out of the oven. She'd run out of yeast, having had to throw away so much bread from the first two batches, and had heard somewhere that bicarbonate of soda could be substituted, so she'd gone to the pharmacy and bought some. Having no idea of what quantity to use, she'd dumped all four cans into the dough. Even if it was too much, she reasoned, it would aid people's digestion.

The baking soda hadn't had quite the effect on people Brigitte hoped for. Symptoms ranged from uncontrollable drooling to red, irritated eyes to abdominal cramping and discolorations of the skin. Pierre, the bar owner, hadn't been able to get rid of his spots for two weeks. Dominique had decided that day that the best course of action would be to try to teach his bumbling, flighty sister some basic pastry-making skills.

"Okay, I'm done," said Brigitte. "But I don't understand how this is going to turn into a croissant in the oven."

Her brother couldn't imagine how either.

"Brigitte. Leave that for a minute and come here." The young woman went to sit next to her brother. "Do you like working at the bakery?" Dominique asked her.

"Of course! I love it. Every day I'm learning more. Whenever you want, I'll be happy to take over for you. If you want to go on vacation, I mean, or just take a few days off."

"Well, we'll see. The important thing is that you like the business. The thing is, things aren't going so well right at the moment." Dominique rubbed his hands together nervously. He wasn't sure how his sister would react to what he was going to propose. "You already know," he went on, "that I'm thinking of expanding production of my heart-shaped sugar cookies."

"I'm sure they're going to be a huge success," Brigitte interrupted. "They come out so perfectly when you make them!"

"I know." Dominique's hand rubbing became more agitated. "The problem is that I'm not going to be able to do it—I mean *we* aren't going to be able to do it—" he corrected himself, knowing how important it was to make her feel she was an integral part of the plan, "—without financing. The bank doesn't want to lend us the money to build the factory, and without funding, there won't be any wholesale production of sugar hearts."

"But you make them so well, I'm sure someone will lend you the money!"

"That's just it!" Dominique exclaimed. Brigitte looked pleased at having hit on the solution. "I'm positive that if I put it to the lottery winner, he would be happy to lend me the money in exchange for a share of the future profits."

"What a fantastic idea, brother!" Brigitte began to applaud, using just her fingers. "But . . . how are you going to pitch your idea to the winner if nobody knows who he is yet?" She wrinkled her brow.

"*You* are going to find out for me," Dominique said, looking at his sister fixedly.

"I don't understand. How am I supposed to find out?" She crossed her arms. "If I at least had an idea of who to ask—"

"You don't know, but *I* know who you need to ask."

Dominique spent the next twenty minutes explaining how he had found out that Father André knew the identity of the lucky winner and describing his unsuccessful attempt to obtain that information. He also said this was his last chance to open the factory he'd always dreamed of and that she was his last resort, the only one he could count on to find out the name of his future investor.

The plan was simple. Brigitte would go see Father André and tell him that through an unfortunate accident she had become pregnant by a boy from another town. She would say that she wanted to keep the child, but that the father was refusing to support her. In order to avoid publicly humiliating her family, it had occurred to her that if she had a good amount of money she could move somewhere else and start a business to support herself and the child. And what better person to lend her the money than the winner of the lottery? Surely he wouldn't even miss a few thousand euros, especially when he had the opportunity to help someone from his own village find a solution to such a terrible problem.

Brigitte listened with her mouth open, nodding continually. Not once did she interrupt as her brother, his eyes alight, explained every detail of the plan.

"Did you understand everything I said?" Dominique asked when he'd finished.

"Perfectly," she said, thrilled to be playing such an important role in the plan her brother had come up with. "When do you want to do it?"

"Right away!" Dominique stood up from the chair he'd been sitting in while explaining his scheme. "Why wait? This is the ideal moment. Father André will have just gotten up from his siesta. If you go there now, I'm sure you'll find him in the sacristy."

"Okay. I'll go now." Brigitte hardly heard herself speak these last words because she was suffering a sudden attack of nerves. It was one thing to talk about it and quite another to carry it out so soon, without even any time to warm up. But maybe it was best to get it over with as quickly as possible. If all went well and she was able to help her brother in this way, he would never forget it. The thought filled Brigitte with pride.

She took off her apron and went to wash her hands. When she returned, she found her brother standing next to a large basket of big yellow peaches.

"I was thinking that if you go see him with the pretext of giving him these peaches, it will be easier for you to initiate the conversation," Dominique said, handing her the wicker basket full to the brim with fruit. "You can say that someone brought us peaches for jam and that you kept these back for him." Her brother raised his eyebrows suggestively.

"Okay, I'll take them to him. I'll let you know how it goes."

She picked up the basket of peaches and left the bakery. A few yards away, she hesitated and looked back. Through the glass display window she saw Dominique watching her. When he saw her, he nodded and gave her a big smile and a thumbs-up.

A Lucky Day

13

The bathroom window was so fogged up that drops of water were condensing on its surface and sliding down the wall, pooling on the old brick floor tiles. So hot it was almost scalding, the water issuing from the shower head had turned the room into a Turkish bath. Julien stood under the stream, scrubbing his back with a brush that was almost two feet long. He hadn't used the brush for quite some time, but this was a special occasion, and he could be sure this way to reach the parts of his anatomy that were almost inaccessible otherwise. His hair was full of the fragrant lather produced by a special shampoo infused with essence of rosemary he'd saved for just such an important moment. Julien had received a small bottle of this shampoo the last time he'd visited the central office of the Postal Service in Lyon. The national Postal Service had organized a three-day continuing education seminar on information technology, consisting of lectures and hands-on workshops. Several companies had taken advantage of the gathering of so many postal workers from the area to hand out free samples of their products, no doubt with the idea that the mail carriers would distribute the samples to the people on their routes, thus providing free advertising for them. A cosmetics firm had given Julien a bag full of face and body lotions, exfoliating creams, potions to combat cellulite, self-tanners, fancy soaps, etc., most of which Julien thought were ridiculous and had no use for. He'd given almost all of them to Madame Babette, hoping they might cheer her up since she'd been mourning her late husband at the time. All he'd kept for himself was the sample bottle of rosemary shampoo. Its fragrance, according to the description, was relaxing and hypnotizing. Julien hoped that meant for others who smelled his hair, not for himself. It would be pretty embarrassing if you went around all day with a dreamy expression smelling your own hair.

He'd stood under the scalding water so long his skin had turned red and gave off steam like a burning log recently extinguished. Drying himself with an oversized yellow towel, he took extra care to rub between his toes, something he didn't normally do. When he fastened the towel around his waist, it hung down over his feet and dragged on the floor. Julien began to wipe the steam off the mirror over the sink with his right hand. Looking at his reflection, he was pleased—maybe it was the shampoo with essence of rosemary, he thought. Standing sideways, he sucked in his belly. Not bad for forty-some years old. He still looked like a young kid.

Julien stood for a minute musing on what Father André had told him about Bernadette. For an instant he vacillated about his course of action. Perhaps he hadn't understood the priest correctly. It was true Father André had already had too many glasses of wine. Maybe he didn't know what he was saying or had mixed Julien up with someone else. Maybe Julien shouldn't have told the priest how he felt about Bernadette in the first place during that forced confession.

She was a married woman, after all, and it wasn't right for him to break up such a long-term relationship.

Father André told me very clearly that she shares my feelings, he thought, chiding himself for his doubts.

He had to carry out his plan. He'd been plagued by doubts ever since leaving the priest at the sacristy, but he'd made his decision and that was that . . . or was it? Julien sat down on the toilet lid, propped his elbows on his knees and dropped his face into his palms, then ran a hand over his hair.

Am I sure about doing this? So much time had passed since he'd made himself stop dreaming about her that now that the opportunity to do something about it had presented itself, he wasn't sure whether to be happy or angry. Bernadette had been a forgotten chapter in his life—well, almost forgotten— and opening the door to those feelings again was causing him great anxiety.

What happens if I tell her I love her and she doesn't feel the same way? I won't be able to bear it. The pain will be so excruciating I'll have to move away from Sainte Marie. I won't be able to face her after that. On the other hand, if the possibility does exist and I don't take advantage of it, I'll never forgive myself.

Heartened by this last thought, Julien stood up and faced the mirror. It had fogged over again in spite of his having opened the bathroom window, and he had to wipe it clean again. He spread a thick layer of shaving cream over his face. Normally he was very careful about how much he used, but today wasn't the day to scrimp. This was followed by a liberal application of deodorant, not just under his arms, but all over his chest. He combed his hair. When the shaving cream had softened his beard sufficiently, he began to shave, using a brand new blade. This was an extravagance, since he hadn't been planning to change the blade for three or four days yet, but his shave needed to be the closest ever today if he was to make the impression he wanted.

Five more minutes were spent brushing his teeth, and finally Julien concluded with a generous spray of a cologne he usually saved for holidays. *Perfect*, he thought, surveying himself from head to toe in the mirror.

Julien left the bathroom and quickly put on a shirt and a pair of cream-colored slacks. He sat down on the edge of the bed to put his socks on and paused, staring at the wall, as doubts began to infest his mind again. Memories of the Saint John celebration twenty years ago suddenly flooded his brain. The dancing had begun, presided over, naturally, by the Orchestra Fantaisie. They had all been so young then, Julien, Bernadette, and Dominique. Even the orchestra members looked as though they'd barely graduated from the conservatory. The only thing that hadn't changed in twenty years were the frilly blue suits the musicians still wore. Dominique and Bernadette hadn't been a couple at that time—all the young people went out together as a group, though some were beginning to pair up. The future baker had been quite a Romeo in his day. He preferred to make his conquests among the young girls who came to spend their summers on the beaches of the French Riviera and had never shown any interest in the village girls. Unlike Dominique and his three other friends, Olivier, Thierry, and Émile, Julien was very timid and rarely left Sainte Marie. Olivier was a local boy who was always up for whatever scheme Dominique invented, no matter how harebrained it might be, while Thierry and Émile were from a town on the coast, but rode their motorbikes to Sainte Marie every day.

One weekend, Dominique had insisted that Julien go to the beach with them, enthusing about the multitude of foreign girls there who were much more interesting than the ones from Sainte Marie. He'd been so persistent that Julien couldn't say no unless he wanted his reputation as a party pooper to become even more firmly entrenched. Going with them had seemed preferable to enduring a summer of jokes at his expense. He'd met several girls, but since his heart already belonged to Bernadette, he hadn't paid them much attention. Dominique had made fun of him, telling him he was hopeless with women and that this was the last time he would be invited to accompany them.

It was then that Julien had committed what he now considered the greatest mistake of his life: to stop Dominique's taunts, he'd confessed that he was in love with Bernadette. Dominique said now he understood many things and had left off pestering Julien, who had interpreted his response as literally meaning that Dominique had understood him and had decided not to bother him any more. Two weeks later, at the Saint John celebration, Julien talked to Bernadette the whole night. His plan was to ask her to be his girlfriend, but his nerves had gotten the better of him and he couldn't find the right moment. He'd invited her to dance the twist, and the two of them had laughed uproariously. They'd continued dancing when the orchestra struck up the next song, a slow one. That had been the moment to ask her; both of them knew it, both of them wanted it and hoped it would happen—until a finger had tapped Julien's shoulder. When he'd turned around, a smiling Dominique had asked Bernadette to dance. Julien had stood there paralyzed, not knowing what to do. He didn't want Bernadette to dance with Dominique, but he didn't want a confrontation either. As he dithered, Dominique took Bernadette's arm and began to dance with her. Julien had stood stock-still among the couples whirling on the village square and watched them as they'd moved away. That was the last time he saw her that night, and the next day he found out from his friends that Dominique had asked Bernadette to be his girlfriend and that she'd accepted. Julien had spent the remainder of that summer closeted in his parents' house, sitting on his bed staring at the wall. Just like he was doing now.

This last thought woke him from his catatonic state. *This time it will be different. No more excuses. I've wasted twenty years of my life living without the woman I love, and I'm not going to waste a single minute more. I'm going to see Bernadette right now, and I'm going to tell her everything I never told her and then*—his mind was on fire—*then, I'll tell her I love her.* An involuntary smile curved his lips and a shiver of happiness ran through him. *I don't care that she and Dominique are married. She'll just have to leave him. I don't care that they have kids either.* He shook his head. *I'll treat them as if they were my own. The only thing that matters is that we love each other.*

Thus determined to change his luck, Julien put on his shoes and went to the front door. There he picked up his keys from the small wooden table that stood in the entryway and looked at his reflection one last time in the mirror above it. He took a deep breath. His life was about to change.

14

July 10

"Hail Mary most pure."

"Conceived without sin." He heard a woman's voice through the wooden screen of the confessional.

A few seconds went by. They weighed on Father André, who hadn't had the chance to drink his accustomed coffee after his afternoon nap and was feeling sleepy.

"My daughter, I can't hear you. Speak." This was too much. He'd been awakened from his siesta to hear an urgent confession, and now the woman was tongue-tied. "Come, the sooner you let it out, the sooner you'll feel better."

"You see, Father, I, the thing is . . ." The rest was inaudible to the priest.

"My child, either you're going to have to speak louder or I won't be able to hear your confession." Father André wondered what this woman could have done that she was so ashamed to confess.

"The problem is that when you can't see things clearly, you can't . . ." Again, the rest of the sentence was lost somewhere between the wooden screen and the priest.

"Madame Babette, speak up or I'll hear your confession another day!" exclaimed Father André sternly, looking around the side of the confessional. In a gentler tone he continued, "Doesn't it seem more reasonable to you that, since I already know perfectly well whose confession I'm hearing, and since you came to wake me up from my siesta, that you should just come over here to this side of the confessional where we can talk more easily?"

"It's that it embarrasses me so much to confess in front of you." The widow was very nervous. Her heart was beating so hard she was afraid it would jump out of her chest. She'd been diagnosed with a serious heart condition after her husband's death, and the doctor had urged her to avoid upsetting situations because they could bring on cardiac arrest. "If you feel your heart is beating too fast, you must relax immediately," he'd warned her. "Otherwise it could be fatal." From that moment on, Madame Babette had tried always to maintain a state of serene composure.

"I understand, ma'am," Father André answered, shaking his head as if to deny the reality of what Madame Babette had just told him. "But you must remember that I'm not here to judge you. I am nothing more than a conduit for the Lord's forgiveness of your sins."

"I know that, Father André, but for me these things . . . What can I say, they've always been difficult for me." Madame Babette was unable to meet her confessor's eyes. She'd been taking deep breaths for some time in an effort to slow her heart rate, and it had finally worked. "You know I've always been very modest my whole life. I never allowed my husband to do anything unless it was completely dark."

What was beginning to get dark was the afternoon, thought the priest. It looked like this confession was going to take a while. Father André had hoped for a lazy afternoon so he could immerse himself in his favorite hobby: painting. A few years ago he'd taken a correspondence course in oil painting, and since then he'd devoted every spare minute to his art. It was more complicated in wintertime because the days were so short, which was why he liked to take advantage of the long summer afternoons to put in at least a couple of hours. He didn't celebrate evening Mass in summer until seven thirty, so he usually had plenty of time after getting up from his nap. Today didn't seem to be his lucky day, though.

"All right, Madame Babette, shall we begin?" Father André cut to the chase. "What would you like to confess, my child?"

"Very well, Father, let's begin." Madame Babette resigned herself. "The other day at the butcher shop they gave me too much change back, and I knew it perfectly well but I didn't say anything."

"Don't worry yourself, daughter. The next time you go you can return it. Just tell Bastian you didn't realize your change was wrong until you got home." Finally they seemed to be getting somewhere. *Let's see how long she takes,* thought the priest.

"I said bad things about a woman from the village at the beauty shop," continued Madame Babette.

"I'm not surprised. That place is a gossip factory, but of course you need to repent of your sin." What would be strange would be *not* to hear malicious gossip in the beauty shop, considering that all the women in the village went there to have their hair done on a daily basis. *It must be impossible to keep your mouth shut in a situation like that*, thought Father André.

Madame Babette went on confessing venial sins. It was apparent she was saving the best for last. The confession about the beauty salon drew Father André's attention to the enormous golden light bulb that soared heavenward from Madame Babette's skull. *Mary's Beauty Shop must go broke on hairspray for this woman's visits*, he thought. *How do they manage to make it so high? It must have wires inside it or something; otherwise it would be physically impossible to maintain a hairdo like that. And how does she sleep at night?* he asked himself while imagining the giant trough Madame Babette's hair must leave in the pillow. Meanwhile, the widow droned on, enumerating her small faults. Father André saw that it was five o'clock. Realizing that his dream of an afternoon of artistic endeavors was quickly going up in smoke, he interrupted her.

"If that's all, my child, pray three Our Fathers and three Hail Marys."

"I haven't finished yet!" she protested. "I still have something to confess," she said, casting her eyes down and giving Father André a view of the top of her beehive.

"Very well. Proceed." The priest looked directly into her eyes. It had occurred to him that perhaps that way she would hurry up a bit.

"The thing is, Father, that two days ago, when I was in the butcher shop, in addition to me not giving back the extra change, something else happened." It seemed that the technique of looking deep into her eyes was working. Father André congratulated himself. "I felt just the way I always do until it was my turn. I asked Bastian for some pork ribs and he went into the back for a minute to change his apron. From where I was waiting, I could see him through the door because he hadn't closed it all the way. He took off his apron and also his undershirt and I saw his strong chest and powerful arms. All of a sudden, Father, I felt a shiver running all the way from the back of my neck down to—well, you can imagine where." She crossed herself. "Mother of God, I can't believe I'm telling you this! The truth is, Father, that ever since that moment I haven't been able to stop imagining Bastian without his shirt on, embracing me—" She crossed herself again. "And with the light on! Every time I think about it my heart beats so fast I feel like it's going to jump out of my chest." She sighed and continued in a more formal tone. "Of course afterwards I feel guilty. That's why I needed to confess so urgently."

Father André was speechless. How was it possible that this sweet little old lady of almost eighty could have such lustful thoughts? He didn't know what to say. Madame Babette had finally raised her eyes to his and was anxiously awaiting her confessor's reaction, but he was paralyzed.

"Is my sin really bad, Father André?"

"It's not a minor sin, my child . . . though of course it is better to sin in thought rather than deed, and to repent of your sin before it goes any further."

"So what penance will you give me?"

"Ten Hail Marys and ten Our Fathers," answered Father André. "And two Creeds . . . and no meat for a month. Or better, two months."

"Very well, Father." Madame Babette dropped her eyes again.

Father André gave her absolution and the widow retired to one of the pews to do her penance. The priest remained inside the confessional waiting for her to finish. She'd given him such a shock he felt incapable of getting up.

When Madame Babette had finished, the priest accompanied her to the door of the church where he sent her on her way, not without reminding her not to eat meat until the fall. Realizing there was still time to paint before the seven thirty Mass, he began to close the door when he heard a voice calling him. "Just a minute, Father André! Don't close the door—I have something for you."

The priest looked up the street and saw Brigitte, Dominique's sister. She was carrying a large basket covered with a white cloth.

"Good afternoon, Father André," Brigitte gasped, out of breath from her final dash to reach the church before the priest closed the door. "I have some peaches that we saved for you at the bakery."

"Thank you very much, daughter. I'll take them, don't worry." The priest planted himself before the door to keep Brigitte from entering. The only thing on his mind now was continuing the still life he'd begun a couple of weeks ago.

"It's no problem. I can carry them in." Brigitte put her foot inside the door, making it impossible for Father André to close it. "Besides, I need to talk to you about something."

Father André glowered at her, and Brigitte wondered whether this was the best moment to carry out her brother's plan, which was pure genius. "If I could just have a few minutes, I would be grateful," she ventured finally.

"All right. Come in and tell me what it is in the patio of the sacristy." Father André grudgingly allowed her to enter, hoping it wouldn't take too long. They walked through the church to the sacristy where the priest lived. From there they went into the courtyard, where the enormous mulberry tree was in full leaf since it was the height of summer. Brigitte had seen the patio in wintertime, and the image of the mulberry, skeletal and leafless, rose in her mind's eye.

"It's amazing how much this mulberry tree changes from winter to summer. It seems like a different tree," Brigitte commented, trying to get the conversation going.

"Yes, it changes a lot," Father André answered dryly. "Go on, set the basket down there on the marble table. When Clément comes I'll tell him to take it to the kitchen. So. What was it you wanted to tell me?" As he spoke, Father André skillfully tied a white apron covered with multicolored splotches of paint behind his neck, then went to his easel and removed the cloth draping it, revealing a half-finished still life. Next to the easel stood a pine box with two metallic clasps that the priest opened, taking from it paints, a brush, and a palette with more splotches of paint on it. Brigitte observed this operation from her seat without saying a word.

"Come on, Brigitte, tell me what it is. I don't have all afternoon!" Father André picked up a tube and squeezed out a fat worm of red paint onto the palette. He flattened it with the brush and began to stir it.

"I didn't know you painted so well, Father André," Brigitte said, using the same tactic she employed with her brother. "You've never mentioned it."

"It's just a little hobby I've had for years. Just a distraction." The clergyman seemed pleased by her words.

To the right of the priest was a small rectangular table covered with a tablecloth that held a basket with plastic fruit, a small pitcher of water, and a glass. The arrangement seemed very tasteful to Brigitte, who really thought Father André had artistic talent. She herself wasn't very good at anything. Maybe that was why she appreciated talent in others more than other people did.

"It's amazing how you make everything look so real," she complimented him honestly.

"Thank you, my child. I've gotten pretty good at still lifes, but what I still have trouble with is live subjects. It's much more difficult to paint the expression on a person's face or an animal's, you know?" Father André had forgotten that he wanted his visitor to leave. He felt very comfortable talking to Brigitte as he painted.

"So then what you should do is practice more with portraits and forget about painting bowls of fruit."

"I'd love to, but the thing is no one except Clément knows I paint." He looked up from the canvas at Brigitte, who had begun to wander around the patio. "He let me paint him one time, but I had to give it up. It was impossible. He couldn't sit still for two minutes. To be a model requires a lot of concentration. You have to be completely motionless for long periods of time, even hours." He looked back at his painting. "So I've resigned myself to doing still lifes."

Meanwhile Brigitte had sat down on one of the chairs next to the marble table and was trying to figure out how she could begin to put her brother's plan into action. Her conversation had made the atmosphere more relaxed, though she was unaware of this. The priest interrupted her thoughts, giving her the opening she needed. "So are you going to tell me what's bothering you?"

Brigitte lifted her face to him and began to talk. She told him the whole story her brother had so recently invented, adorning it with so many details that at one point she began to believe it herself. Realizing it made the story more believable, she started to imagine her characters' faces and, from time to time, inserted real details that even Father

André would be familiar with. She told the priest, for example, that her imaginary boyfriend had come to Sainte Marie for the St. John celebration and there they'd argued. The priest had seen many young people from other towns on that night in particular and had no reason to disbelieve her. Brigitte told him that her unborn child was the most important thing to her and she wasn't going to allow anyone to harm him. This was an agreeable surprise to the priest, given the tender age of his visitor.

Brigitte finished speaking, lowered her head, and hugged herself. Father André could have sworn he'd seen tears in her eyes.

"Are you all right, my child?" The priest went to her and stroked her hair. "Don't worry. You've made the right decision. Everything will be all right." He took her in his arms and held her until she regained her composure. They sat down at the table.

"I just don't want to make my family suffer. I need to confront this on my own. That's why I came to you."

"Don't worry about a thing. I'll do everything I can to help you."

Now entirely calm, Brigitte went on with her story. Never had she had a more attentive audience than Father André, and she knew it. She explained her idea to him and how he could help her right the wrong that had been done. All she needed was for him to tell her who had won the lottery.

"But my daughter, I don't know who the winner is. I'm afraid I can't help you there."

"But you hear confession from everyone in the village. You must have arrived at some conclusion from listening to what the townspeople have to say. Surely you have a theory about who the winner is. I'd love to hear it."

"I can't talk about what people tell me in confession, it's a very serious sin." Father André felt the nape of his neck beginning to sweat. He took out a handkerchief and blotted it. The times he'd made little slips—as he called them—rose in his mind. But that had nothing to do with this: purposely telling someone what someone else had confessed. "There's no way I can help you with that."

"But if you help me this way, it won't be a sin because you'll be doing it for a worthy cause." Brigitte gave him a small smile. "I'm not going to tell anyone. All I'll do is go see the winner and discreetly make him aware of my problem. Even if he refuses to help me, I won't say a word to anyone else. If he won't give me the money I'll find some other way to get it—but I'm sure he will. After all, it would be a good deed."

Father André was sweating more profusely now. Brigitte made a convincing case, true, but still, he mustn't betray something he'd heard in confession. On the other hand, if he just gave her his opinion, maybe that wouldn't be a sin . . . and besides, it *was* for a worthy cause. He still felt conflicted about it, though; it seemed something was still missing that would make his decision justifiable. But what could it be?

"I'll make a deal with you, Father André." The priest stared at her, riveted. Maybe this would be the deciding factor that would make it all right. "If you tell me everything you can about the lottery—without compromising the sanctity of the confessional, of course—I'll let you paint me all afternoon."

"What are you saying, my child?" Father André almost stuttered over this simple phrase.

"I'm saying that if you tell me what you know, I'll pose for you this afternoon."

Father André thought for a few moments, his gaze lost in the crown of the mulberry tree. He couldn't see anything wrong with her proposal; he would tell her everything he could if it would help the poor girl in her troubles, and besides, if she would allow him to paint her, it would be magnificent. He'd been longing for years to paint the human form, and here was his opportunity. He lowered his gaze, met Brigitte's eyes, put his head to one side, and said, "All right. But no one can know about this."

"No worries, Father. I'll never tell." She got up from her chair. "Where would you like me to pose?"

"The best place would be just in front of the mulberry, between the light and the shade." Father André got up and walked quickly to the door leading into the house. "I'll be right back. I'm just going to get a new canvas."

The priest rushed into the house and up two flights of stairs, taking them two at a time. When he'd almost reached the top of the second flight, he tripped over his cassock and fell forward on all fours, banging his forehead against a step. Fortunately, he'd put out his hands to break the fall, so the impact wasn't serious. Jumping up, he entered the attic, whose wooden floor also served as the ceiling of the second story. Originally designed as a dry place to store sacks of grain, it had been used as a chicken coop as well after Father André had had an argument with the butcher and resolved to raise his own fowl. They had roamed freely around the attic, but made such a racket that the priest had soon changed his mind. Now it was again used for storage. Books, furniture, and many of the priest's earlier paintings were heaped up everywhere. Father André found the canvases and picked out one wrapped in brown paper that he'd set aside. Canvas in hand, he went down the stairs, more carefully this time, and crossed the sacristy to the patio door.

"Jesus, Mary, and Joseph!" The canvas fell from his hands

when he saw Brigitte. She was waiting by the tree, as he had instructed her to, but had taken off all her clothes and was entirely nude. In her left hand she held a peach from the basket.

"My Lord, Brigitte, please cover yourself!" Father André turned his head away from her as he spoke, looking instead toward the still life. "What were you thinking?"

"But Father, all the models pose in the nude. There's nothing wrong with it. I was thinking that since I'll lose my figure after I have the baby, I would like to be immortalized as I am now, so I can always remember how I looked."

Brigitte's intention, which she seemed to have achieved, was to put Father André in such a compromising position that he would have no choice but to tell her everything he knew about the lottery. Her brother had told her to find out who the winner was, and she couldn't fail him.

"I don't think it's a good idea, Brigitte." Father André was really sweating now. "Imagine if someone were to see us, what would they think?"

"Father, we're in your home, and there's no reason anyone should bother us. If someone knocks, I'll just get dressed really quickly." Peach in hand, Brigitte continued to hold the pose she had assumed.

"Well, I don't know . . . maybe just for a little while. It's true it would be good for me to do some whole-body practice." He scratched his head. "Muscles are difficult to paint."

"Come on, Father André, begin. I'm standing as still as a statue, just like you said to."

"All right, I will." The priest removed the still life, picked up the easel, and set it down in front of his new model. He put the blank canvas on it and brought over his paints and brushes. "But for the love of God, Brigitte, don't ever tell anyone about this."

"Don't worry, Father. I can keep a secret better than anyone. Now, while you paint, tell me what you know about the lottery and who you think the winner is."

The priest began to talk while making a preliminary charcoal sketch. When he reached the pubic area, he turned his eyes away again, not even wanting to imagine having to paint it in detail.

A Lucky Day

15

August 24

Noé leaned his forehead against the rear window of his mother's car, feeling the cool glass against his skin. It was an agreeable sensation. He rolled his head from one side to the other so he could feel the coolness against his temples. When the glass had warmed up so he could no longer feel the difference in temperature, he glued his lips to the glass instead and blew, inflating his cheeks. His brother, who was watching him from the other side of the back seat, couldn't take it any more. His right arm shot out and he rapped his little brother on the back of the head.

"You stupidhead! That hurt!"

The baker, seated in the front passenger seat, tried to turn around to see what was happening, but the seatbelt yanked him back into place and he could only turn his head. "What's going on back there?" he said, glaring at his older son. "Why did you hit your brother? You're too old to be messing around like this in the car. Always the same old thing." He sighed.

"He was getting the window all full of spit!" protested young Dominique.

"I don't care what he was doing! Stop bugging him. You're distracting your mother, and I'm not in the mood for this kind of crap today." Dominique Sr. turned his eyes forward again, then glanced at Bernadette.

"Wow, great way to discipline your younger son," Dominique Jr. said. "He'll never learn to behave that way."

"What?!" His father unbuckled his seatbelt, turned around, and cuffed his older son on the head. "That's all I need, for my son to be telling me how to bring up my children."

At this, little Noé couldn't resist making a face at his brother, which earned him a cuff from his father as well.

"Ow! What did I do?" Noé burst into tears.

"That'll teach you not to make fun of your brother. And not to get the windows of the car dirty." Dominique Sr. turned around again and refastened his seatbelt.

Bernadette had contributed nothing to the discussion. She was angry with her husband, who had insisted that the children spend the night at his sister's house. He had told her there was sure to be some kind of disturbance in the village because of the lottery. Today was the final day for the winner to claim his prize and Dominique, along with several of his friends, was planning to stand guard in case anyone tried to sneak out of town. He was going to be in and out of the house all night and he didn't want the children to be awakened. His wife was annoyed, not understanding why this meant she had to stay alone in the house. Though she very much enjoyed her solitude during the day, at night she got frightened if no one was with her, and the children kept her company. On top of this, Dominique's obsession with finding out who had won the lottery made no sense to her. It had become a mania with him that was beginning to take its toll on their marriage. It wasn't so much that they didn't get along; Bernadette had just known for years that her husband didn't love her any more. Her intuition told her there had been other women, and God only knew how hard she'd tried to forgive and forget, but she was beginning to ask herself what she was doing with this man.

"I don't want to spend the night at Aunt Brigitte's," Noé piped up. "Why can't we stay at home?"

"What's the problem with Aunt Brigitte?" his father asked. "You've always liked being with her. Didn't you say she always makes up really fun games?"

"That was when we were little, but now she just puts us in front of the TV and goes to another room," Dominique Jr. put in. "Besides, her cooking stinks."

"Eww!" seconded Noé.

"What a pair of gourmets," muttered the baker without turning around.

Silence fell during the final few minutes of their trip to Brigitte's house. Though Dominique knew Bernadette was in a bad mood, he made no attempt to lighten the atmosphere. For the baker, his wife wasn't worth the trouble, which, in his opinion, put her on par with every other member of the female sex. Ever since he was a young man, he'd had no trouble attracting women. His looks helped and when he wanted to he could turn on the charm. It was expected that a man of his stature would be married, and marriage was a convenient way to have children, but he saw no contradiction in continuing to chase other women with his friends. He told Bernadette he had to work late at the bakery, and occasionally that was true, but most of the time it was just an excuse to go to other towns and party the way he had when he was young and single.

The car drew up in front of the old house that had belonged to Dominique's parents and where Brigitte now lived. Both siblings had inherited equal shares of the house, but Dominique allowed his sister to live there as if it were her own. Hearing the car, Brigitte came to the door while her brother got out and opened the back door for the kids.

"Come on, out!" He shook his finger at them. "And give your aunt a kiss."

The children said goodbye to their mother, got out of the car, and went inside after giving Brigitte a kiss at the door. Dominique went up to his sister and kissed her on the cheek. "Thanks for keeping them. I hope they don't give you too much trouble."

"Don't worry, they always behave themselves." She peered at the car and saw Bernadette sitting behind the wheel. "What's up with her? Grumpy again?"

"You know how she gets sometimes. It'll pass. Nothing to worry about."

"Be careful tonight. There have already been too many problems. You don't need any more trouble, Dominique."

"Relax. Nothing bad's going to happen. The only thing that can happen is that the winner will finally show himself." He looked into her eyes and gave her another kiss on the cheek. "That's what we've been waiting for since the beginning. Now get inside and see what my two savages are up to."

Brigitte waved goodbye to Bernadette, who returned her wave. The baker walked back to the car and opened the door. As he was climbing in, his sister called again, "Be careful, Dominique!" He waved at her and got into the car.

Bernadette didn't say a word on the ride home. For his part, Dominique, fed up with his wife's bad moods, didn't attempt to converse either, knowing it would gain him nothing. As they drove along the mill road, they caught up to Julien the mailman, who was pedaling slowly along. Bernadette felt envious when she saw him. She wished she could be on that bicycle too, instead of in this car next to a man she no longer loved. They passed Julien too quickly to say hello, nor did they want to. The poisoned atmosphere that filled the car made it impossible. Right when their white house came into view at the end of the road, drops began to spatter the windshield. The rain came on rapidly and in no time it was pouring. In spite of it being barely six o'clock in the afternoon, the sky turned so dark it seemed night had fallen.

When Bernadette parked, the rain was coming down so heavily they couldn't even see the front door, only a few yards away. They got out and ran toward the house. Bernadette stopped at the door and took off her shoes so as not to track mud into the house, but her husband walked right in. Bernadette watched him disappear down the hall, leaving a trail of muddy footprints on the blonde parquet. Her eyes reddened and began to puff up. She tried with all her might not to give her husband the satisfaction of seeing her cry, but the tension that had built up in her overwhelmed her. Bernadette held out for almost ten seconds before dropping to her knees and crumpling to the floor, sobbing.

Dominique put his head around the corner. "Time for another drama?" he said, approaching his wife. "You're unbelievable. When it's not one thing, it's another, just as long as you manage to make my life a living hell. What's wrong with you this time?"

"I can't do it any more, Dominique! What's wrong with me is you! I've tried, God knows I've tried as hard as I can." Bernadette had never imagined the day would come when she could actually express her feelings. "I've stayed for the kids, not for you, but I can't do it any more. I don't want to keep on fighting to save this farce of a marriage that never should have happened in the first place."

The baker's face went rigid. He couldn't believe what he was hearing. Until that moment he'd always believed that his wife didn't really think about their marriage. Without knowing why, he was suddenly invaded by panic. He had to handle this situation right.

"Darling, you can't really feel that way. We love each other." He came closer and tried to take her in his arms. "I understand, you've been under a lot of pressure. We all are because of the lottery. I love you, my darling."

Bernadette pushed him away when he tried to stroke her hair. "Get away from me! You don't love anyone. Or maybe I should say the only person you love is yourself. You think I don't know about your other women? At least you've had the decency not to get involved with someone from Sainte Marie."

"What are you saying, my love? You're the only one." He again tried to hug her. "Where are you getting this?" Dominique was more concerned now with finding out who had gossiped to his wife about his exploits than he was with calming her down. "Who told you those lies?"

"A woman doesn't need anyone to tell her these things. She just knows. There are signs."

"Signs?" Dominique was beginning to get irritated. "Don't tell me you're making a scene based on 'signs'?" His tone turned from honeyed to sarcastic. "You're insane."

Bernadette began to cry again. She was sick to death of being humiliated, but there was nothing she could do. Dominique was her husband, after all. She asked herself who would put up with a woman her age with no career and two children from another marriage.

Dominique went on. "What you need to do is occupy yourself with the house and the boys and stop imagining 'signs.'" He made quote marks with his fingers. "Don't you realize I'm the one who supports this household? What have you ever done for me aside from making my life impossible? You've been good for nothing your whole life. I don't even know why I asked you to dance that night. I would have been better off if you'd stuck with Julien. He was crazy for you and now he would have been the one having to put up with your complaints."

"What do you mean, Julien was crazy for me?" Bernadette stopped crying all of a sudden and stood up. "That night when you asked me to dance you told me Julien didn't like me and that he had another girlfriend. You told me he made fun of me and all he wanted was to take me to bed."

"It was a long time ago. I don't really remember. No doubt it was the way you say." Dominique realized he'd put his foot in it badly. He'd always been careful never to mention that night to his wife or to Julien. He'd even told the mailman that the only reason Bernadette hung out with him was so she could be closer to Dominique, the one she was really in love with.

"So my whole life with you has been based on a lie?" Furious, Bernadette shoved her husband toward the door. "Get out. I never want to see you again. I hate you!"

"You're a real nutcase, you know? I'm going to stand guard and wait for the lottery winner." He grabbed an umbrella and a raincoat from the coatrack next to the front door. "We'll talk tomorrow when you've calmed down. You're probably on your period. Everything's always a tragedy during those days."

He left the house, slamming the door. The rain was still pouring down. Dominique opened the umbrella and ran for his wife's car. Meanwhile, inside the house, Bernadette fell to her knees again. She wanted to cry, not from sorrow but from rage, but she couldn't. She was done crying over her marriage. Feelings of relief and happiness filled her as she realized Julien hadn't betrayed her. Suddenly all her worries coalesced into one: would she be able to convince Julien that none of it had been her fault?

Ding, dong! Ding, dong! The doorbell rang twice. Dominique must have forgotten something. Bernadette couldn't stand the idea of seeing him again. She hadn't had time yet to assimilate everything that had just happened. But she screwed up her courage; she would need it to face the coming collapse of her world. She would let him in, but without continuing the conversation. It had all been made crystal clear already. Bernadette sat up, reached for the doorknob, her heart beating fast, and opened the door.

Before her, looking like a drowned rat, stood Julien. His shirt and pants were soaked and drops of water slid from his hair onto his nose and chin, falling from there to his shoes, also squelchy with rainwater.

Bernadette didn't have the chance to say a word or explain anything. Julien took her in his arms and kissed her as

CARLOS J. SERVER

Dominique never had, and she allowed herself to be kissed. "Julien, I . . . there are so many things I want to explain to you."

"Hush. I've been standing outside the door for the last few minutes and I heard everything." He kissed her again. "I've never stopped loving you."

"And now what?" Bernadette's voice trembled.

"Everything that happens from here on out can only be good."

A Lucky Day

16

July 11

The days were growing hotter, but temperatures at night were still chilly. This resulted in higher levels of condensation and dew-drenched dawns. Roads were wet, as if it had been raining all night, and water dripped from the trees, forming small puddles beneath.

Dominique put on the wipers, as he did every morning, to clear the windshield of the bakery van. He preferred winter to summer. It was colder but at least he could sleep in a little more. Since people didn't get up so early, he was able to open an hour later.

He was always the first to arrive at the bakery. He allowed Brigitte to sleep in a couple of hours longer on the condition that she remain in the bakery over the noon hour so Dominique could go home for lunch and a siesta. But today was different. The baker hadn't been able to sleep a wink all night because his sister had gone to visit Father André the day before to worm out of him the name of the lottery winner. Dominique had waited all afternoon for her to report back, but hadn't heard a word. He'd even caught himself doubting her. After several unanswered calls, he'd thought about going to her house, but after a long discussion with Bernadette he'd decided to wait until the next morning.

Unable to stand the suspense a minute longer, Dominique left home an hour earlier than usual and went directly to his parents' house, where Brigitte lived. As he drove up, he realized he'd left his keys at home. He could have rung the doorbell, but Dominique knew it would be useless. From a very early age, his sister had been a light sleeper and always used earplugs. Once she put them in, she couldn't hear a thing. Even an alarm clock didn't wake her up.

So she wouldn't always be late to work Dominique had bought her a special clock that gradually increased the light in the room as the hour to wake up neared. Today, though, it would be another three hours until the clock went into action, so the baker pressed his finger to the doorbell and simultaneously called Brigitte's home phone. After fifteen minutes of this two-pronged approach, he gave up, realizing he would have to think of another solution. He walked around the house, scrutinizing it, and saw that the window of his sister's bedroom on the second floor was half-open. Maybe he could climb up the façade of the house? Without thinking twice, he drove the van to the side of the house and climbed on top of it. This put him within range of the ledge that ran along the façade, separating the first and second stories. Reaching up, he began to climb, propping a knee on the ledge. It was slippery with dew, though, and his knee slipped off. His pants snagged on something, and when he pulled himself up again, the fabric tore, leaving his left leg completely exposed.

Once he'd gotten both feet on the ledge, Dominique stood up, his back pressed against the wall, feeling the chill air on his naked leg. He looked down and thought that maybe what he was doing wasn't such a good idea after all. If he fell or got hurt, there would be no one to help him, since everyone in the village was still asleep.

He looked in the direction of the church bell tower and saw a shadow moving at the end of the dark street. At first Dominique thought it was a tree until he saw it advancing toward him. As the shadow approached, it took on human form. It was Jean Baptiste, the man who irrigated the local orchards. There was nothing odd about him walking through the village this early, since water was available twenty-four hours a day. In one hand he held a hoe, and in the other, a small overnight bag, faded and stained with mud. Dominique didn't fully recognize him until the man was in front of his parents' house. He went as still as a statue, hoping Jean Baptiste wouldn't realize he was standing on the second-story ledge. He didn't want to have to explain why he happened to be in such a strange location. After all, in a village the size of Sainte Marie d'Azur, this was the sort of situation that would be delightedly hashed over by all his neighbors the next day. Dominique held his breath, but the irrigator looked up and saw him anyway.

"Good evening, Dominique. What are you doing up there?"

"Good evening, Jean Baptiste. I lost my keys and was hoping I could get in through that window on the other side."

"Oh, I see. Well, good luck. I must be getting on. I need to water the garden at the mayor's country house." He took a couple of steps and turned back. "Have you tried the front door? Sometimes it's open and you don't realize it."

"Uh, no, I haven't. I haven't tried it, but I don't think it's open."

Jean Baptiste walked up to the door and turned the knob. The door opened. "I told you! That's happened to me several times."

"I can't believe it," Dominique muttered under his breath, adding in a louder voice, "What do you know? Thanks!"

"Don't mention it. Would you like me to help you down?"

"That won't be necessary. Please, don't let me hold you up. I'm sure you're in a hurry." Dominique was mortified and only wanted the man to leave as quickly as possible. "I'll climb down myself."

"All right, have a good night, then. By the way, have you noticed your pants are torn?" Jean Baptiste said, standing under the ledge. "Be careful coming down. Everything's very slippery from the hoarfrost."

"Yes, I'm aware of it, thank you, Jean Baptiste, and I'll be careful. You needn't linger any more. Good night to you."

"Good night. Goodbye." The irrigator went on his way, a shadowy figure that disappeared into the night much as he had appeared. Dominique descended carefully from the ledge onto the roof of his van and from there to the ground. He stood looking at the open door for a moment, unable to believe what had just happened. Shaking his head, he went inside.

The interior of the house was black as pitch. Dominique couldn't see anything, but knew the layout well, since the house had belonged to his parents. He struck out confidently, but after two steps, his bare knee hit a piece of furniture, sending a needle of pain shooting through him. Shaking his right hand, he smothered a yelp. As his eyes adjusted, the furniture around him materialized in the gloom, giving him the feeling he was in a different house. He hadn't remembered this arrangement. Retracing his steps to the doorway, Dominique felt for the light switch. Again he was blinded, this time by the light instead of the darkness. Though this was his parents' house, everything looked different because his sister had changed the furniture around.

Dominique went up the stairs to Brigitte's bedroom. Entering the half-opened door, he saw his sister asleep, curled around her pillow.

"Psst, psst! Brigitte! Wake up." He touched her shoulder.

Brigitte gave a little scream. "Who is it?!" She sat up instantly and began to punch Dominique's head.

"What are you doing?! It's me, Dominique!" He grabbed her wrists to stop the blows.

"What are you doing here?" Brigitte's heart was pounding. "Why on earth would you just show up without calling first?"

Dominique couldn't believe his ears. This, after having torn his pants, bashed his knee, and now, had punches rained on his face? "Come on, wake up! We have to talk. Didn't we agree you were going to call me yesterday after you'd seen the priest?"

"Well, it got late, and since I know how early you get up, I didn't want to disturb you."

"Get up and get dressed. I'll make some coffee and wait for you downstairs." Dominique got up from the bed and went downstairs.

A few minutes later, Brigitte descended the stairs. The aroma of fresh coffee rose up to meet her, banishing the irritation she'd felt about her brother waking her up so early.

They sat down at the kitchen table. Brigitte related to her brother Father André's initial reluctance and how she had convinced him to tell her everything he knew. Naturally, she didn't mention anything about the painting.

"Good. That's good," Dominique said, beginning to feel impatient. "But who is the winner?"

"Father André doesn't really know for sure. He says no one has confessed specifically to being the winner, but he has his suspicions. From everything he's seen and heard, he thinks it may be Bastian."

"What Bastian?" Dominique asked, perplexed.

"What Bastian do you think?" Brigitte looked at her brother. "The butcher."

"Bastian? Impossible." Dominique stared incredulously at his sister. "If it were Bastian, I would know about it. Why would he want to hide it?"

"Father André says he knows for a fact that Bastian has been planning a trip to the Seychelles Islands at the beginning of August."

"That can't be. Bastian always goes to see his family in Nord Pas de Calais in August. He's done that his whole life, ever since he was little. He always used to go with his parents."

"Well, this time he's going to Seychelles. Two weeks ago, Carmen, the woman who cleans Bastian's house, found a folder in a desk with first-class tickets, a reservation confirmation for a luxury hotel, and a complete tourist guide to the Seychelles Islands."

"I can't believe it! Bastian?" Dominique was dumbfounded.

"Also, Father André told me that Seychelles is on the list of countries that are tax havens. So Bastian's planning to take his money there, no doubt. That's the last we'll see of him."

"What are you telling me?" The baker's eyes were like saucers.

"Father André had suspected others, but he says that if he had to put money on someone, it would be Bastian. He told me he wouldn't put his hand in the fire, of course, but all the evidence points to him." Brigitte was thoroughly enjoying having her brother's attention riveted on her. "I'll spare you further details because I don't want to bore you, but it all adds up," she pronounced.

"This Bastian is trying to fool us all by just leading his normal life and then planning to disappear forever." Dominique's expression went from incredulity to rage. "We can't allow it!"

"What are we going to do, brother?"

"If it were anyone else, I would talk to him discreetly, but Bastian needs to be taught a lesson." Dominique's eyes lit up. "Let's tell the others and give him a little scare so he'll listen to reason. That money's staying in this village."

"What will you do to him?" The sinister expression on her brother's face was making Brigitte nervous.

"Something he'll never forget."

A Lucky Day

17

August 24

Seated on the floor, Charlie was coloring in a notebook. He had drawn a tree with a thick trunk with lavender-colored birds posed on its branches and a huge lavender-colored sun above. Around him, Father André and the boy's parents were having a spirited conversation. They had decided to move from the patio to the house since it had begun to rain hard a while ago.

The priest studied Charlie's drawing. "This boy really has artistic talent," he told the parents. "And that's an educated opinion."

"He does love to draw," said Jeanette. "Every day when he gets home from school, the first thing he wants to do is color."

"That's wonderful," said Father André.

"It also helps us to discipline him," put in Adrien. "If he

doesn't want to pick up his toys or brush his teeth, we just tell him he won't be allowed to color and it works like a charm."

Father André laughed at the little boy's innocence. Though the last few months had been hard, it cheered him to think that life went on, and Charlie was proof of it. "By the way, why does he color the birds and the sun purple?" The boy's choice of colors was surprising. As strange as the result was, though, the colors harmonized well.

"It's not purple, it's lavender," Jeanette corrected him. "Charlie loves lavender. It's his favorite color and he always uses it in his drawings."

"Does that seem strange to you, Father?" Adrien asked in a worried voice. "It's never seemed normal to me."

"Don't worry, my son." The priest got up and placed his hand on Adrien's shoulder. "We've all got our eccentricities. The good thing about this one is that it's not hurting anyone."

Jeanette smiled at her husband and caressed his left hand. Meanwhile, Father André had gone to the window, bent down, and looked up at the sky that was getting darker by the minute.

"It seems to be raining harder than before," he commented to the couple. "But don't worry. These summer storms are very showy but they don't last long. It would be better for you to wait a while for it to let up."

"We don't want to bother you," Jeanette replied. "You've been so kind to us. Besides, you must be celebrating Mass in a little while."

"It's no bother. On the contrary, I'm happy to have company this afternoon. I prefer to have you here rather than to think of you possibly getting into an accident because of the rain. And don't worry about the Mass. With this rain, I don't think many people will show up. It will just be the four of us—maybe a few others."

Adrien and Jeanette looked at each other, wordlessly agreeing that they must stay to attend Mass, especially after the priest had been so kind to them.

Outside, the rain continued to fall. The sound was pleasant to Jeanette. She sipped a little water and gazed at Charlie, who, heedless of his surroundings, continued to draw lavender birds.

A Lucky Day

18

July 15

The clock in the bell tower was about to strike eight p.m. The minute hand had begun to tremble, an unmistakable indication that within a few seconds it would move to its highest position.

Waiting impatiently on the sidewalk, Madame Babette straightened her blue blouse so it wouldn't crease. A light breeze lifted a pleat of her skirt, affording a glimpse of her embroidered slip. She smoothed her beehive obsessively; she'd been at the salon early that morning and didn't want the wind to muss her hairdo.

No sooner had the clock begun to chime the quarter-hours than the door of the butcher shop opened and two women came out with a child. Madame Babette looked at her watch, oblivious to the church clock that was striking eight. In spite of having loitered more than ten minutes on the sidewalk across from the butcher shop, she attempted to give the impression that she wasn't waiting for the last customer to leave. The little boy who had just come out—he couldn't have been more than nine—stared at her without blinking. Madame Babette crossed the street toward the shop and the boy turned his head to follow her progress. In contrast, the two women chatted without paying the least attention to the widow. For a moment, it seemed to Madame Babette that that boy knew her secret. She averted her eyes in shame and then dismissed the idea as impossible. Stepping up onto the sidewalk, she pushed open the door.

"Good evening, Madame Babette," Bastian greeted her with a smile. "What a beautiful day today, eh?"

"Very nice, I must say," answered the widow. *The day was nice too,* she thought.

"You almost missed me. I close at eight, but I don't mind staying late for you." Bastian went to the door and turned the "Open" sign around. "This way no one else will come in. Today I have some things to do at home. What can I get for my best customer today?"

"Oh, Bastian, you're going to make me blush." Nervous, she smoothed her hair. "I'm sure you say that to all the ladies."

"I do—and they all believe me." They both laughed. "But when I say it to you, it's the truth. Some day you must explain to me how you manage to put away everything you buy from me."

"I don't buy that much." Madame Babette was attempting to prolong the conversation as long as possible.

"How can you say that? You come in every day."

"It's just that your meat is really . . . good." She wondered how she could have said that aloud. Her hands flew to her hair again.

"All the products we sell in this butcher shop are top quality," Bastian responded cheerfully, completely unaware of the bent the conversation was taking. "What can I get for you today?"

"Oh, I don't know, I don't know. Could you give me a few of those veal chops? They look so good." Madame Babette knew precisely what she wanted and it wasn't veal chops. "Would you mind deboning them for me? I know it's more work for you, but it's for a recipe I saw in a magazine at the beauty shop."

"No problem. We aim to please."

"Thank you, Bastian." Madame Babette smiled and added, "My dear."

The butcher took out a couple of knives and began to sharpen them. The sight of Bastian stropping the knives was quite a treat for Madame Babette. She imagined those strong arms lifting her and carrying her around the room, and such a powerful shiver ran through her that even Bastian noticed.

"Are you cold, Madame Babette?" he asked. "I need to keep the air conditioning on high so the meat stays fresh, but if you'd like I can turn it down."

"No, I'm fine, Bastian, don't concern yourself. Maybe I caught a chill tonight," she said, inventing an excuse.

Bastian set the knives down and went to the air-conditioning unit, turning the control to the left. "In just a moment it will be better." He went back to the knives, adding with a smile, "We don't want our favorite customer to get sick."

At his smile, the widow trembled again, but this time the butcher didn't notice. After carving the meat to her specifications, Bastian placed it on a white Styrofoam tray and, without wrapping it, held it over the counter for her inspection. "Does it look all right?" The sight of the tanned, firm muscles in the butcher's arms mesmerized Madame Babette. "What do you say? Nice pieces of meat, no?" Bastian looked into her face.

The widow couldn't tear her eyes from those arms. They definitely looked like nice pieces of meat to her. The question *how many things could he do with those arms?* popped unbidden into her mind. She extended her hand toward them, actually brushing the butcher's flesh.

"Careful, Madame Babette, remember they're not wrapped up yet," Bastian warned.

She awoke from her fantasy, jarring the tray with the back of her hand. The chops fell onto her blue blouse.

"Mother of God, your blouse!" Bastian ran around the counter to her. "I'm so sorry! It was my fault."

"Don't worry, it's all right." Madame Babette didn't know what to do. She wanted to clean herself up, of course, but wasn't sure how to do it without getting even dirtier.

"I'll pay the dry-cleaning bill or the cost of a new blouse." Bastian was agitated. "Let me bring you some towels, or better yet, why don't I take you to the restroom? You'll find supplies there to clean yourself better."

Bastian accompanied Madame Babette to the restroom. The image of the widow, with her huge bulb of platinum hair and her hands held up reminded him of a B movie about extraterrestrial aliens invading the earth. Bastian opened the door for her. "Here are towels and whatever else you require. I'll be here in case there's anything else you need."

Madame Babette appeared to be in shock, mutely continuing to hold her hands up. Bastian closed the restroom door and went back to the front of the butcher shop. Chiding himself for his clumsiness—no one was more aware than he of how difficult it was to get blood out of clothing—he told himself he must be more careful in the future. He carved new chops for the widow, wrapped them up securely and placed the package in a bag, adding some chorizo and one of his special Majorcan sausages for good measure. When he finished, he turned off the lights in front, leaving on only the ones in the back of the shop. Approaching the restroom door, he asked, "How's it going, Madame Babette? Do you need anything?"

"No, don't worry," he heard from the other side of the door. "I'm almost done."

Bastian put his hands into the pockets of his smock and walked slowly back to the front of the shop, now illuminated only by the streetlamps outside. When he reached the counter he looked up and saw two men wearing black ski masks.

"What's the meaning of this?" Bastian frowned. "What do you want?"

"So this is the famous Sainte Marie d'Azur butcher shop," said the taller of the two men. "I imagined it would be bigger."

"If you're looking for money," Bastian put his hand into the cash register drawer and took out a few bills, "there's not much here, but it's all I have."

The tall man spoke again. "I see you have no problem handing over your money to us. Maybe you've got too much money."

"I don't understand. What are you saying?"

The other man went to the door, drew the bolt, and stood with his back to the door in the middle of the shop. The taller man seized Bastian by the collar of his smock and dragged him to where the other man was standing.

"Please, don't hurt me! Take whatever you want!" Bastian was on the verge of tears.

"We're only going to hurt you a little," said the second man, who hadn't spoken up to that point. "Just enough to make you understand what you should and shouldn't do." He gave Bastian two swift kicks in the stomach. The butcher writhed with pain on the floor. He brought his hands to his head instinctively, but the tall man pulled them away and pressed his shoe into his face. Bastian began to tremble as the man brought his mouth close to his ear.

"Listen carefully because I'm only going to explain this once," he said in a low voice. "Blink to show me you understand."

Bastian processed the man's meaning quickly and blinked.

"We know you're a lucky man, but that fortune has to be reinvested here. The money's not leaving this village. What happened here tonight can be a one-time thing; it's up to you. If you want everything to be normal again, you need to be generous with your neighbors." The man suddenly shouted, "Is that clear?"

Bastian was at a loss. His rational mind told him he needed to blink again to get out of this mess, but he hadn't understood a word of what the masked man had said. He decided blinking was his best option and did it.

"That's good, butcher. I see you're a quick learner." The man took his foot off Bastian's face and the two pulled him to his feet.

"Now, butcher, we'll take that money you offered us," said the other man, the one who had spoken least.

Bastian went to the cash register and picked up the bills he'd dropped minutes before when the man had attacked him.

"We're leaving now," said the tall man. "Naturally, you're not going to say a word to anyone about what happened here tonight, and you're going to do everything we said."

"Just to be clear," Bastian interrupted in a low voice, "what I'm supposed to do is be generous with the people from the village, right?"

"Exactly," said the shorter man.

"Okay . . ." Bastian said, "but generous how? This business doesn't leave much for extras."

"Are you making fun of us?" the taller man asked.

"No, never!" Bastian began to tremble. "I just wanted to make sure it was clear."

"Look, butcher," the taller man went on. "What you need to do is spend the money you won in the lottery here in the village, not on some weird island, got it?"

All of a sudden, like a lightning bolt to the brain, Bastian understood. These men thought he had won the lottery, but they couldn't be more wrong. He never even played! Why would they think he was the winner? And why were they demanding the money stay in the village? If they were really thieves, they would have tried to steal the prize money from him. Instead, they wanted him to invest it in Sainte Marie. There was something very strange about all this.

Madame Babette's voice sounded from the back. "I'm finished. I couldn't get it all off, but almost—"

Bastian had forgotten the widow was in the restroom. Now she would come out here and find herself face to face with the masked men. Guilt flooded him and he regretted delaying their departure with his last questions. He would never forgive himself if they hurt Madame Babette because of him.

The masked men tensed when they heard her voice. One of them positioned himself behind the door to the back of the shop and signaled to Bastian to keep quiet. When the widow came through the door, the butcher shouted, "Run, Madame Babette!"

She had no time to react. The shorter man grabbed her from behind and covered her mouth with his hand. On the other side of the counter, the taller man stepped up to Bastian and punched him in the face, knocking him to the floor.

"Don't hurt her!" He looked at his attacker. "Don't you realize she's elderly? Let her go! She has nothing to do with any of this."

Bastian's words hurt Madame Babette more than the arms imprisoning her chest. Her heart began to race. She needed to calm herself; the doctor had warned her that any acceleration in her heart rate could be harmful, even lead to a heart attack. The widow tried to take a deep breath, but her attacker was holding her so tightly that she couldn't. She tried to struggle against him, but it was impossible; the more she tried to get away from him, the tighter he squeezed her. Her heart pounded in her temples, faster and faster until she couldn't distinguish between the beats. An unbearable pain ran up her left arm and the butcher shop grew vague and hazy. Her legs buckled.

"She fainted!" said the man who had been holding her. He sat her down on the floor and moved a few yards away from her. "Now what do we do?"

"We'd better get out of here," said the tall man.

Bastian scooted over to Madame Babette and propped her in a sitting position against the wall.

"And don't forget, butcher. That prize stays in this village," the tall man said, lifting his index finger. The two thugs ran out of the shop.

Bastian held Madame Babette's wrist and took her pulse. It still beat. He searched in her bag until he found a small silver-plated pillbox. Inside he found what he was looking for, the widow's nitroglycerin tablets. Since the death of her husband, everyone in the village knew that Madame Babette suffered from heart problems. She had made sure to tell them all what to do in case she suffered a heart attack one day: place a nitroglycerin tablet under her tongue. Bastian had never paid much attention; her admonishments reminded him of the safety announcements on planes about what to do if the plane went down over the water or where to find the life jackets. It had never occurred to him that one day he might be the one to administer this remedy to Madame Babette.

Exercising utmost care, the butcher opened the widow's mouth and placed the pill under her tongue. "Come on, Madame Babette, wake up!" He held her hand, praying silently that she would open her eyes. She moved her head slightly and Bastian smiled. "Come, look at me!" He wanted more of a reaction than that.

Barely moving her lips, Madame Babette murmured, "Bastian, is that you? What happened to me?"

"Relax, Madame Babette. Rest." Bastian smiled, got up, and ran to the door. Opening it, he began to shout for help. Some men at the end of the street heard him and ran towards the butcher shop.

"Call an ambulance, quick!"

One of them stopped and turned around, while the other

kept running. A woman came out of one of the houses across the street to see what was happening and rapidly went back in to call the emergency number.

Bastian re-entered the shop to see how the widow was doing. He took her hand again and, out of breath from shouting, asked how she was feeling.

"I'm all right now." Bastian could barely hear her.

"You'll see how quickly you feel better. Don't worry."

Madame Babette looked at her hand, saw that Bastian was clasping it in his, and felt much better already. She tried to squeeze his hand, but was too tired. She could feel his pulse, though, and it was calming.

"Bastian," she murmured. "Whatever happens, don't let go of me."

"Don't you worry. I'll stay with you."

Madame Babette's hand stopped moving. She had closed her eyes and her pulse was much weaker now. "Quickly! Get the doctor!" Bastian yelled at the top of his lungs. His eyes, reddened already by rage, began to well with tears.

The minutes crept by. Neighbors came into the butcher shop and watched in incredulous silence, but without doing anything. Finally the door opened, admitting the doctor who pushed his way through the crowd. Approaching Bastian, he took a stethoscope from his black bag and applied it to Madame Babette's chest.

"How is she?" asked Bastian.

"Her pulse is very weak," replied the doctor.

"But she'll be all right, won't she?" insisted the butcher.

"I don't know, Bastian." The doctor turned to look at the butcher. "Let's hope she has something to live for."

Bastian gazed at Madame Babette and squeezed her hand. The sound of a siren grew louder.

A Lucky Day

19

August 24

A thin sheet of water covered the asphalt of Main Street. The impact of the raindrops on this surface produced tiny bubbles that made the water look granulated. The day had been hot, even hotter than usual for Sainte Marie d'Azur in August. The rain from the unexpected cloudburst began to form rivulets, and as the water flowed over the hot black pavement puffs of vapor rose into the air, making it feel even more sweltering.

A red car was parked at the intersection of Main Street and the highway, its windows completely steamed up. Three men had taken refuge from the rain inside, smoking and carrying on a lively conversation.

"Hey, do you guys remember the Italian girl Dominique picked up last summer?" asked Olivier. "I think she was the ugliest dog I've ever seen in my life."

All three laughed uncontrollably, remembering the event.

"He's always had a weakness for Italian girls," Pamphile went on. Still laughing, he added, "Whatever they look like."

Everyone burst into renewed guffaws. Olivier was crying, he was laughing so hard.

"Where did he get that obsession with Italian girls?" asked Thierry.

"Dominique always said the Italian girls were much more interesting than the ones from around here," answered Olivier. "Especially, as he says, if they don't know any French—if you get my meaning."

If it hadn't been for the drumming of the rain outside, their laughter would have been heard up and down the street. Thierry, calming down a bit, turned on the windshield wipers to see what was going on outside, but the glass was so steamed up he couldn't see a thing. Pamphile, in the front passenger seat, turned on the defrost.

"What's up, Thierry?" he asked. "You look worried."

"I've got a weird feeling, a premonition." Thierry's unusual height always made him feel cramped whenever he was in a vehicle. "I just feel like something's going to go wrong," he added.

"But why? Everything's peaceful," said Pamphile. "It's all in your head. Forget your premonitions. It's all going fine so far."

"Things have gotten so bad, it would be better if no one tried to leave town today—they might not make it out alive."

Their friend's remark sobered the others. Helping Dominique out was one thing and having a death on their hands was quite another. They'd already had a taste of that in the butcher shop with that old lady. She'd almost died when all they'd meant to do was frighten the butcher.

The windshield had cleared enough by this time to make

out a car approaching from the end of the street. Thierry and Pamphile stared at it. "Okay, guys, out!" said Thierry. "Let the show begin."

They all opened their doors and got out at once. Each wore a large plastic trash bag with a hole cut in it for his head as a makeshift raincoat. As the car continued down the street in their direction, Pamphile's heart began to race in his chest and he couldn't get Thierry's remark—*they might not make it out alive*—out of his head. He'd almost forgotten the incident at the butcher shop, but he wouldn't have wished on his worst enemy the sleepless nights he'd spent worrying that Madame Babette might die and he and Thierry would be accused of homicide.

When the car was about thirty feet from them, Olivier exclaimed, "It's Dominique, in his wife's car!"

They all watched as the vehicle parked in front of their own. Pamphile gave a sigh of relief at the sight of his friend. Dominique killed the engine, got out of the car, and walked toward the group.

"What a day we got, huh?" he said. "No doubt a premonition of how it's going to go for the lottery winner when we catch him trying to leave town."

"Didn't I just say?" asked Thierry.

"But it's better if he does show up, right? So we can take his ticket," Olivier said.

"We can't take the ticket from the winner, Olivier, how many times have I told you that?" said Dominique. "What we can do is convince him to give us part of his winnings in exchange for us letting him leave town. Right, Thierry?" The baker nudged his tall friend with his elbow.

"Yeah, and that part's getting larger by the day." Thierry

nudged him back. "For our trouble, I mean." The two men laughed and Pamphile and Olivier joined in halfheartedly.

Dominique cut them off. "But we have to be careful. On my way here I saw Sergeant Chardin out patrolling in his cruiser."

"What's that fatso going to do?" Thierry scoffed. "Helping little old ladies across the street is about his speed."

"I'm not worried about Chardin per se," replied the baker. "What I don't want is for him to get nervous and end up calling the Gendarmerie in Cannes."

As he spoke, the patrol car swung onto Main Street and headed their way.

"Speak of the devil," Thierry said.

" . . . There he is!" added Olivier, laughing. The others didn't find it quite so funny.

The cruiser reached the end of the street and pulled up next to them. Without getting out of the car, Sergeant Chardin rolled down the window and stuck his head out. "Good afternoon, gentlemen," he said.

"Good afternoon, Sergeant," said Dominique, who had walked up to the driver's door.

"Hello, Dominique. Don't you think with all this rain, you'd all be better off in your own houses?" Chardin asked, his face stern.

"We all just happened to run into each other here, so we were just shooting the breeze for a while," Dominique answered.

"Look, Dominique." The sergeant frowned. "I don't think

you're getting my meaning. I want all of you to go home right now."

Dominique lifted his head and looked at his companions. He would have liked to give a different answer—who was Chardin, a small-town cop, to think he could take that tone with him?—but his final objective was more important right now. He would deal with the sergeant later. "Don't worry, Sergeant, we'll be on our way soon," he said. "Just five more minutes. It's not really worth it to be out on a day like this, I agree." Dominique leered at Chardin like a hyena.

"All right. I'm going to continue my rounds, and I'll expect you to be gone by the time I get back here." Without waiting for confirmation, the officer rolled up his window and continued on his way. Dominique had to jump back to avoid having his foot crushed by the back wheel of the cruiser.

"When all this is over, Chardin's going to get his," said Thierry in a tone that gave Pamphile goosebumps.

"No worries, bro," replied Dominique. "I know just how you feel, but the important thing right now is to get our hands on that ticket."

"How are we going to do it if we can't stay here?" asked Olivier. "You heard Sergeant Chardin."

"We'll split up. Thierry and Pamphile will stay here in their car, and you come with me, Olivier. We'll park in front of the post office," Dominique ordered. "We'll stay in the cars so we don't have trouble with Chardin. When someone comes along, stop him. You can say the highway's closed because of a landslide caused by the rain. That way no one will attempt it. Since you guys aren't from here, people will believe you. If anyone's attitude seems suspicious or they act overanxious to get out of town, call us and we'll come right away.

Understood?"

Everyone nodded and followed the baker's instructions. Olivier got into the car with Dominique and they drove off. Thierry and Pamphile climbed into the red car again. The windows fogged up immediately. Pamphile reached toward the dashboard to turn on the defrost, but Thierry batted his hand away.

"Stop! Don't you see, if you do that they'll see us," he scolded his friend. "Just clean off a little spot and keep watch that way. That's all we need, for that cop to come back."

"You're right. Sorry."

"Anyway, if that fatso dares show his face here again, he'll get what's coming to him," Thierry said pointedly without taking his eyes from the peephole he'd made on the glass.

Pamphile said nothing. He looked at his friend and the words *they might not make it out alive* resounded in his head again. A chill ran up his back and he had to squeeze the nape of his neck to relax the tension building there. He turned around and brought his face close to the window, hoping no one would try to leave town that afternoon.

20

July 20

Every Saturday, an hour before the service began, Father André would seat himself in the confessional so that anyone who wished to confess his sins before God could do so. Normally very few people showed up until shortly before Mass started, so the priest usually brought a book to entertain himself with while he waited. Though he knew perfectly well probably no one would show up for the first forty-five minutes, he still enjoyed the peace that reigned in that small space. Besides, on hot days like this one, it was much cooler inside the church than in his rooms or the sacristy.

Inside the confessional, Father André had installed a small reading lamp precisely so he could read while he waited. The soft light given off by the lamp seemed to reinforce the relaxed atmosphere. Today the priest had chosen a book on nineteenth-century oil paintings. Clément had given it to him for his birthday and he hadn't had time to enjoy it yet.

Father André passionately perused the pages. In his opinion, the painters whose work appeared there were true artists, capable of reproducing the essence of whatever subject they painted, animate or inanimate. His opinion of painters from later periods differed markedly; he didn't understand how the later movements could be so much more widely known when all those artists relied on artifice. Needless to say, for Father André, that wasn't painting.

Each and every one of the works he saw reproduced in the pages of the book astonished him. He considered them all amazing. The book was organized alphabetically by painter, and he leafed through Anderson, De Beruete, Boldini, and Corot, sighing at the magnificence of their work. When he got to Courbet, he was struck dumb by a painting entitled *Still Life with Apples and Pomegranates*. The strokes the painter had used to render the fruit were masterful. The still life he himself had been working on for so long was similar to Courbet's composition, so the priest studied the colors and shadows carefully. What caught his attention most was the way the artist had painted a glass containing some sort of infusion. *Really sublime*, concluded Father André silently.

He turned over the page and found another Courbet painting, this one called *The Painter's Studio*. It depicted the artist working on a landscape while a white cat lay at his feet. Watching him were a small boy and a model who attempted unsuccessfully to cover her nakedness with a white robe. Father André thought of his session days earlier with Brigitte. It had been a unique opportunity to paint the human form, though he mustn't repeat it. Since that day he'd had the feeling that the Lord's eyes were on him, watching him constantly. He stuck his head out the side window of the confessional and looked at the cross hanging from the altar. "Lord," he murmured, "that wasn't right, but there was no evil in it, You know that." He turned his eyes back to the book and turned the page, nostalgia for the painting he'd just looked at already tugging at him. When he got to the next painting, however, he slammed the book shut and crossed himself. The Lord must be testing him. He slowly opened the book to the same page. *It's just a book, and besides, I didn't write it,* he thought.

The final Courbet piece the book contained was called *The Origin of the World.* The priest couldn't get used to such a strange origin. The painting was of a nude woman lying on a bed, her face covered by a sheet. Her legs were open and all her female anatomy was on display. To the old village priest, the only thing in that nonsensical painting that made sense was the fact that the model had covered her face with the sheet. He couldn't imagine what would have become of that woman if she'd shown her face. How would people have looked at her in the Paris marketplace?

He was so absorbed in his thoughts about the painting that he didn't realize someone had come into the church to confess. When a shadow fell over the book, he closed it quickly and whirled around.

"What was that you were reading, Father André?" Bernadette asked him, unable to believe her eyes. "Aren't you ashamed? At your age . . . and you a priest! What will people think?"

"What a fright you gave me, my child!" exclaimed Father André, shaken. "It's not what it looks like; it's a book of paintings."

"Erotic paintings, judging by what I saw," Bernadette replied, kneeling on the other side of the confessional.

"Not at all!" answered the priest indignantly. "It's a book on nineteenth-century painting that the sacristan gave me. As you would expect, it includes paintings of nude women."

"What I saw looked like more than just a painting of a nude woman, Father."

"Do you have something against paintings of nudes?" the priest defended himself nervously. "The human body is the most natural thing there is, and we shouldn't be afraid to show it or contemplate it."

Bernadette's expression clearly expressed her disbelief at what she was hearing. When Father André saw this, he added, "I'm speaking from a theoretical point of view, of course. My interest is purely academic . . . because painting is my hobby, you know?"

"Very well, Father André. We'll pretend I didn't see anything and begin again."

"I agree, my child." He sighed.

"Hail Mary most pure," said Bernadette.

"Conceived without sin," answered the priest. "What do you wish to confess?"

"Well, you see, Father, because of recent events I've been thinking a lot of things over." For a moment Bernadette wondered whether she should continue with her confession.

Her voice trailed off and Father André urged her to continue. "Tell me, daughter, what's worrying you?"

"After what happened at the butcher shop, I've been worried about never being able to have a truly fulfilling life. I don't know if I'm making myself clear, Father."

"Not very, truthfully," he answered. "But please go on."

"Take Madame Babette, for example. After the death of her husband, it seemed she'd lost the will to go on living, but she bounced back. She found new hopes and dreams to live for. She went from being depressed to being the jovial person we all remember her as, with her multicolored brooches and her perfect hairdo that always looks as if she just got out of the beauty salon. Then all of a sudden, that thing happened in the butcher shop and gave her a heart attack." Bernadette paused again. Just when the priest opened his mouth to comment, she added, "I don't want to end up like that, Father."

"Okay, let's take this a step at a time," interrupted the priest. "To begin with, Madame Babette is doing much better and is going to recover completely. I spoke to the doctor this morning, and he told me it's very likely she'll be discharged next week. So we'll be seeing her around town again soon with her brooches and her hair."

"You don't know how happy it makes me to hear that. I was very worried."

"All right. Now, you can't compare yourself to an elderly lady who has suffered from heart problems for years. You're in the prime of your life, with two adorable children and a husband who loves you."

"That's exactly the problem," Bernadette interrupted. "My husband doesn't love me."

"How can you say that?" asked Father André, alarmed. "He works so hard to make sure all your needs are met."

"It's true he works a lot." Bernadette reflected for a moment before going on. "But it's also true that he doesn't work any harder than I do with the house and the kids. I may not get paid for it, Father, but my work is very hard too."

"Of course, my child, I understand. I know that's true. But I'm sure you won't deny that, just like with many other couples, it's only fair that if one works outside the home, the other should take on a greater share of the work at home."

"That's not what I'm talking about, Father. I'm very happy being a housewife and bringing up my children. The problem is that my husband thinks I don't do anything, that I just lie around all day or . . . who knows what. I don't understand who he thinks is doing the cleaning, cooking, setting the table, taking care of the kids." She stopped herself again, her eyes red, then continued. "He has no respect for me, Father."

Father André sighed. He'd seen many matrimonial crises during his long years in the village, and this was just one more. Nothing that couldn't be resolved with a few well-chosen words of encouragement. Of course, he would have to talk to Dominique about pampering his wife a bit more, but he felt confident things would right themselves in the end.

"Besides, my husband is unfaithful to me." The words dropped like stones from her lips.

For the priest, these words changed everything. This was no longer a simple crisis of self-esteem, it was something much more serious. When you added unfaithfulness to the mix, things were different. Father André understood what Bernadette felt like doing, but he was also well aware of the consequences of a separation for a family. He needed to handle this situation with utmost delicacy.

"Let's see, Bernadette. How do you know your husband is deceiving you? Are you sure your suspicions aren't unfounded?"

"I've had my suspicions for years; I would say they were more than suspicions—there were signs. But now I know for sure. A few weeks ago, I was cleaning out a desk we don't use much. One of the drawers was stuck, and when I jerked it, it came out and everything fell on the floor. It was a bunch of papers, mostly letters and bank receipts, but I also found an envelope with personal letters in it. They were handwritten by a woman named Annette, and it was very clear that she was having a relationship with my husband."

"Are you sure, Bernadette? Remember, jealousy is a bad counselor."

"If you want—" Bernadette began to cry.

"Calm yourself, child. You'll see, it will all work out."

Bernadette took a deep breath, opened her bag, and fished for a handkerchief to dry her tears. Taking out a sheet of paper, she gave it to Father André.

"If you want, you can judge for yourself."

Father André took the letter and sat back to read it.

Dominique, my love,

I'm writing you because I didn't get to say goodbye in person. I was hoping to be able to see you this Saturday. Your friend Thierry told me you had to go to Germany for work and that you were sorry you hadn't been able to see me again. The days we spent together this summer were unforgettable. You made me feel desired again and I'll never forget your caresses. I hope to see you again next year, but if you want you can write to me. You know my address; it's the same as the last time you were in Rome with your friends last year. What memories . . .

Forever yours,

Alessandra

Father André finished the letter, folded it, and handed it back to Bernadette, thinking all the while of what he was going to say to her.

"It's clear this woman had a romantic relationship with Dominique, but couldn't it have been when he was young?" Father André had found an argument. "There's no date on the letter, after all. It could have happened before you were married."

"I also found these photos in the envelope." She handed them to the priest.

The pictures showed Dominique embracing a blond woman. Some had been taken on a nearby beach that Father André recognized immediately, and others in Rome—the monuments in the background were unmistakable. One photo even showed the two of them naked in bed. All the pictures had been shot with a camera that automatically recorded the date, and were from the current year and the one before. With this last proof, there could be no doubt of a guilty verdict.

"You're right, my child. Your husband has deceived you." Father André took Bernadette's hand in his own and went on. "The important thing, though, is that you still love him, and you're going to fight for your marriage."

"No, Father," she responded. Father André drew his hand back. "I don't love him. There was a time when I thought I did, but I was just lying to myself. Now that I've been thinking about it, I don't think I've ever loved him. I did appreciate him in certain ways, yes, and besides he was very handsome, and that attracted me to him. But love him? No."

Her confessor sat motionless, without a clue as to how to proceed. Fortunately there was no need, because Bernadette kept talking. "When I was young, I loved another boy. He was the one I really cared for. I thought he would be the love of my life, but he lied to me as well." She sighed again. "As you can see, Father, that's the story of my life, men that lie to me. Though I never fully understood what happened with that one—I thought we were made for each other. One day, out of the blue, I found out he was cheating on me, and from then on, he never tried to get close to me again. It was really weird, but I guess it was the typical story of what might have been, but didn't work out in the end."

"Tell me more about that story. I'm interested." Father André was beginning to put two and two together with what Julien had confessed to him weeks ago.

"There's not much more to tell, Father."

"Who was that boy?"

"Julien. The mailman."

"Oh, I see. Of course." The priest understood now.

"Why do you say that?"

"No reason. I'll tell you later. First tell me what happened with Julien."

"Okay, Father. If you're that interested, I'll tell you." Bernadette smoothed her hair back, propped her elbows on the confessional ledge, and began. "Ever since we were little we were always together. When we got older, I confess that I began to feel more than friendship for him. One year, at the St. John celebration, just when I was hoping he would ask me to be his girlfriend, I found out he was going out with someone else. At first I couldn't believe it—I kept waiting for him to explain—but after that night, he never talked to me again, the whole summer. He probably found out that I knew everything and was too ashamed to come and explain. I would have understood and forgiven him; he was the love of my life, after all. The strangest thing about the whole affair was that I've never seen him with another woman. Whenever I see him now, I always think about what my life could have been if I'd married him. Father, I'm so unhappy."

"Sometimes life closes the doors we think are the right ones so we'll open others that will be better for us." The message Father André wanted to give Bernadette had become clear to him now.

"What do you mean? I don't understand you."

"You should listen to your heart. Things are often not what they seem . . . even though they are in Dominique's case." The priest vacillated for a moment about whether he should continue to emphasize the importance of preserving the family at all costs, but realized that in this instance, the scales were tipped too far in favor of Julien and Bernadette. "Not all men are the same. If there's something in your mind that doesn't add up, I urge you to clarify it. You may be surprised."

"So then, I should forgive Dominique?"

"No!" the priest exclaimed. "I mean, of course we must always forgive our neighbor, but what you need to clarify is why you're with the wrong man. If you really want to definitively close one door and open another, I urge you not to be afraid to do it."

"I'm not sure, Father . . ." Bernadette was beginning to understand what Father André was trying to say.

"Have faith, my child." He took her hand and smiled at her. "The Lord works in mysterious ways."

21

August 24

The rain continued to pour down on Sainte Marie d'Azur without mercy. An occasional bolt of lightning lit up the bedroom with the sudden brightness of day. From M. François's earliest childhood, the sound of the rain had been the best possible sleeping pill. When he couldn't sleep, which lately had been the case much more often than he would have wished, he would imagine that it was beginning to rain outside in an effort to relax and let himself fall into the arms of Morpheus. The mayor spent his nights wishing for a storm. Now that he had one, though, M. François found he still couldn't fall asleep. Maybe the lottery business had frayed his nerves too much during the last three months—which, to him, had seemed more like three years.

Another flash of lightning turned night into day for an instant. The mayor thought it must be the biggest of all since the storm had begun hours before. He turned away from his wife and squinted at the digital alarm clock. Its weak green phosphorescent light read 10:24. M. François sighed and squeezed his eyes shut again. He and his wife were in the habit of going to bed during the workweek no later than ten p.m., but that night they'd decided to turn in a little earlier.

The electricity had already gone out a couple of times because of the rain, and before bedtime, M. François had put a new battery into the alarm clock so he could unplug it. He preferred to have only those appliances that were absolutely necessary plugged in during storms because of possible electrical surges. What he hadn't foreseen, though, was that when the alarm clock was powered only by batteries, the numbers stayed illuminated continually—one more reason he couldn't get to sleep.

His mind strayed to his orchards. This had been a good year for figs, better than normal. In fact, his fig yield was higher than he could ever remember it, and prices were better this year than they had been recently as well. He just hoped there would be no hail tonight. M. François pictured the fruit pocked and pitted on the branches. That would be the last straw after everything that had happened that summer.

A sudden deafening crack snapped him out of his musings. The thunder following that last lightning bolt was so loud the windowpanes rattled in their frames. The mayor propped himself up to see if his wife had been awakened by the thunder, but Madame Léonore slept placidly on at his side. He felt affronted by this and even more tense, if that was possible. With this storm, how could she go on sleeping as if nothing were happening? M. François reflected on this last thought. Even if it was true that what was raging outside was only a violent storm, couldn't it also be interpreted through the lens of all that had happened in the village during the previous months? For a moment this seemed like an intelligent analogy, but then he rejected the idea as ridiculous, the fruit of a sleep-deprived brain that was going crazy.

He turned back to check the clock again: 10:27. *How can it be possible only three minutes have elapsed?* the mayor wondered as he pulled the sheet over himself. He ordered his mind to go to sleep, but his mind refused to cooperate. M. François decided that even if he didn't sleep and the whole next day was a disaster, at least the deadline for collecting the lottery prize would be behind them.

This thought made him feel more relaxed. At last the nightmare would be over and his village could go back to being the way it had been before. The villagers would be happy, the community united, and he would once again be able to hold his head high as the mayor of Sainte Marie d'Azur when he went to the meetings of the local group of municipalities. Not like the last few meetings, when he'd had to swallow his pride after having boasted so much about being the mayor of the luckiest village in Europe. Once the news had reached them that the prize hadn't materialized and the townspeople had begun to confront each other, his colleagues from the other municipalities had started to bid him farewell with an ironic "See you later, Mr. Lucky Mayor." All that would soon be forgotten, though, and M. François would be able to stick his chest out once more.

Little by little, the sound of the rain soothed the mayor and he began to slip into sleep. Tomorrow was going to be a wonderful day. His mind emptied of thought and everything faded to black.

Brring! The telephone rang. The alarm clock read 10:35. M. François couldn't believe it. Just when he'd finally managed to fall asleep! He pushed back the sheet, sat up in bed, and picked up the phone from his nightstand.

"Yes?" Between the sound of the telephone and her husband's irritated tone of voice, Madame Léonore finally woke up.

"What's wrong, François?" she asked, moving to his side of the bed. "Who's calling at this time of night?"

M. François gestured to her to be quiet.

"Speak slower, please! I can't understand you," exclaimed M. François. He listened for a few seconds. "What's that you say? You have the lottery ticket?"

22

July 24

Julien parked his bicycle in the doorway of the butcher shop, managing to hook the left pedal over the curb in such a way that the bike stood up on its own without having to lean it against the wall. Picking up a large padded manila envelope, he pushed on the door, but found it locked. After a couple more tries, he knocked on the glass. Bastian came into view with his apron on and turned the key in the lock to open the door for the mailman.

"Hi Julien, I'm closed," he said, starting to take off his apron. "If you don't mind, could you come back this afternoon? I've already turned off the machines."

"It's okay, I haven't come to buy anything. I brought you the book you ordered. It arrived this morning."

"Fantastic! Come on in," Bastian said, opening the door wide. He pulled his apron over his head and went to the back to wash up. Julien entered and stood waiting for him with the envelope in his hands.

"I've been carrying it around since first thing in the morning!" Julien called, raising his voice. There was no

155

response.

After a few minutes, Bastian emerged from the back of the shop, impeccable.

"Let's have a look at this baby," he said, approaching Julien.

Julien handed him the envelope. "I was just saying I've been carrying that book around all day. I was waiting until two o'clock to bring it to you so we could go have a beer at Pierre's."

"Sure thing," Bastian said, opening the envelope. "But first things first. I've been waiting a long time for this book. I told you—"

"—that it's a limited edition that was only printed in a few countries in South America," the two men finished in unison.

"You've told me that a hundred times, Bastian. Open it up so I can see this book! You've got me intrigued."

Bastian unwrapped the contents of the envelope carefully, lifting out a book of at least a thousand pages titled *Sin-shar-ishkun, the Last King of Ninime*. He quickly leafed through it, his eyes lighting up as they raced over the index. Julien watched him with a smile, trying to guess why the book was so important to the butcher, but aside from its formidable size and weight, of which he'd been well aware all morning, he couldn't see much else to recommend it. It didn't even have pictures or maps. Just words, one after the other, for a thousand pages. *What a bore,* thought the mailman.

"Hey," Julien interrupted Bastian. "How about that beer?"

"All right, let's go." Bastian left the book on the glass display case. "It's on me today. I finally have something to be happy about this summer."

"I won't say no to that."

They left the butcher shop. As Bastian turned the key in the lock, Julien asked, "Any news about Madame Babette?"

"Yes, she seems to be recovering well," said the butcher. Julien noted something strange in the way he answered.

"Is anything wrong, Bastian? You seem a little down. You know you can talk to me about anything."

"No, nothing's wrong. I'm just a bit tired today, and what happened to Madame Babette affected me a little."

"Well, don't worry. The important thing is that she's getting better. We'll have her back in the village in just a few days."

They walked toward Pierre's bar while Julien recounted something that had happened to him that morning. It wasn't at all interesting to Bastian, but the mailman seemed to find it very amusing. Suddenly Bastian stopped short. Julien walked on a couple of steps before realizing his friend wasn't with him. He stopped talking and looked back at the butcher.

"What's wrong, Bastian?" Julien fixed his eyes on him, waiting for an answer. "And don't tell me you're worried about Madame Babette."

"Two days ago, Dominique came to my house with three of his friends. My daughter had gone to bed and I was watching TV with my wife when they knocked on my door. You could see they'd been drinking. To keep them from making trouble in my house I agreed to take a ride with them. They said they wanted to talk to me. I just thought they wanted to have another drink."

He fell silent for a minute, remembering the events of that night, while Julien watched him and waited.

Taking a deep breath, Bastian began to talk again. "I was wrong. They took me to a vacant lot. The tallest one began to shove me around while the others laughed. Dominique asked me about the lottery prize. He thought I was the winner. I told him again and again that I never even played. I asked where he'd gotten such a ridiculous idea, but they kept getting more aggressive. The tall guy was really out of control. They didn't believe me. They'd found out I was going on a trip and thought I was planning to take the money and invest it in some offshore tax haven. Me—a tax haven! The only money I've got is in a regular savings account!"

"What did you do?" Julien was really frightened, as if what had happened to his friend were happening to him.

"Since they didn't believe me, they decided we should go see Pierre to find out if it was true I never played the lottery. So we went to Pierre's bar, but it was closed already. Dominique insisted on going to his house. I told them it would be better to wait and go the next day, but they wouldn't be dissuaded. When we got to his house, all the lights were off, but the tall guy pounded on the door until Pierre came out. He was really annoyed about being woken up. I was trying to figure out how to get him to say I didn't play the lottery. Then it occurred to me to ask him to open the bar so I could buy a lottery ticket. I told him I wanted to do it that very night. Naturally he told me I was crazy and to wait until the next day. I repeated that I needed to do it right then. For a moment I thought he was going to punch me out, but finally he asked me why I was so interested in playing now if I'd never played before. When I heard him say that I could breathe again for the first time that night. I looked at Dominique, and I could see from his face that he'd gotten the message. Finally I admitted to Pierre that he was right and said I was sorry, that we'd had too much to drink that night. Dominique and his buddies left in the car—the tall guy was driving—and I walked home. I couldn't sleep the whole night thinking about what those animals could have done to me."

"My God!" exclaimed Julien. "Why haven't you told anyone about this?"

"It gets worse." The mailman looked at him in astonishment, waiting for Bastian to explain. "I think two of the guys with Dominique were the ones that came into the butcher shop the day Madame Babette had the heart attack."

"The muggers?"

"No, I lied about that," confessed Bastian. "They weren't robbers; they came to intimidate me and force me to admit I had won the lottery. I have no idea why Dominique and his henchmen believed I was the winner."

"What you're telling me is really serious, Bastian. We should talk to the mayor before these people cause another incident. Madame Babette almost lost her life."

"That's why I'm so worried. I don't know what to do. They threatened to hurt my family if I told anyone." Bastian was suddenly nervous. "Julien, please, promise me you won't tell anyone. You have to promise!"

"All right, I won't tell anyone, but this can't end here."

"It has to! It's better to just drop it!" Bastian was getting worked up.

"Relax. Don't worry, it will all work out." Julien put his arm around the other man's shoulders. "You'll see, the winner will come forward soon and the whole mess will be forgotten. Now let's go get that beer."

"Right. Let's go."

In silence, they continued walking to Pierre's, but as they entered, they froze. Dominique and Olivier were leaning against the bar, drinking. Bastian tried to turn around, but Julien steered him to a table and asked Pierre for two beers. Dominique turned at the sound of the mailman's voice and then continued his conversation with Olivier, pointedly ignoring them, though his eyes never left Bastian.

Seated at the table, Bastian was growing edgier by the minute. He wanted to confront Dominique, but held back for fear of reprisals against his family. It wasn't that Bastian was afraid of the baker. He knew that if he stood up to him, Dominique would cave in; his swagger was all just bravado. On the other hand, Bastian hadn't liked the attitude of Dominique's tall friend when he'd encountered him in the butcher shop and when he'd come to Bastian's house. Julien, well aware of what was going through his friend's mind, chattered on and on, recounting amusing experiences he'd had during his years as a mailman. Little by little Bastian relaxed and began to smile at the mailman's stories. Pierre came over to hear them as well and the three of them ended up laughing hysterically.

Meanwhile, at the bar, Olivier was trying to remember a joke he'd heard, but Dominique wasn't listening. He couldn't block out the laughter from the nearby table and it was really beginning to get on his nerves. Finally, unable to take any more, he turned around and called to the bar owner, "What's going on, Pierre? Do you have to be somebody special to get waited on in this place? We've been wanting another glass of wine for a while now!"

"Be right there," answered Pierre offhandedly. "Just hold on, he's almost done telling the story." He added in a low voice to his companions, "Those guys have been drinking for an hour. Let them wait a little. Go on, keep on with the story!"

When he saw that Pierre made no move to get up, rage began to build inside Dominique. Olivier watched him fearfully. The baker's eyes were bloodshot and he clutched his empty glass as if he wanted to shatter it. Julien finished his story, provoking a resounding laugh from Bastian that filled the bar. Dominique smashed his glass down on the bar and yelled, "I want more wine!"

Everyone stopped laughing. "Coming," Pierre said, rising to his feet. Bastian glared at Dominique. The baker, seeing he'd managed to intimidate the other customers, grew cocky.

Ignoring Bastian's murderous expression, he asked, "What's your problem?" and added, "You weren't having quite so much fun the other night. Maybe you'd better get home. You'll feel calmer if you're with your wife and daughter."

At the reference to his family, Bastian sprang to his feet, strode to the bar, and grabbed Dominique by the shirtfront. "You mention my family again and you'll regret it," he shouted, shaking the other man. "Do you understand?"

"Calm down, man. We're among friends here," the baker responded.

"I've had it with your stupid crap about the lottery. Don't you dare come near me again. That goes for my family too, got it?"

"Let go of him, Bastian!" Julien stood up and tried to separate them, pulling at Bastian's forearm to get him to let go of Dominique.

"Maybe you'd better listen to your little friend," said the baker.

"Come on, leave him alone," Julien insisted. "Can't you see he's drunk?"

"Shut your mouth! You're nothing but a useless village

mailman. You don't have any idea how much liquor I can hold."

"You're a disgrace to your wife and children. You don't deserve them," Julien answered scornfully.

"And who deserves my wife? You, I suppose? You wish. The good little mailman."

"I'm embarrassed for you. You don't know how lucky you are," Julien replied, grabbing Bastian's arm again. "Come on, Bastian, let him go. He's not worth it, can't you see he's an idiot?"

"Wake up and smell the coffee—you never had the slightest chance with Bernadette. You're the idiot. You don't even know what a woman is." Dominique started to laugh.

"You bastard!" The retort came from the bottom of Julien's heart.

Bastian slowly released the baker. Olivier, who had been petrified with fear until he saw Bastian walking away, hurled a parting insult after him. "Watch your back, butcher!"

Suddenly all hell broke loose. Bastian exploded and lunged at Olivier, trying to hit him. Olivier bent down and scooted under the butcher's arm. Dominique took advantage of this to throw a left hook at Bastian, who jumped back to avoid the blow. The one who didn't see it coming was Julien. Dominique's fist connected with his nose, which immediately began to spout blood. Pierre waded in to separate them and stopped the fight. Dizzy from drink, the baker kept swinging his arms around.

"That's what you get for being a smart-ass, little mailman," Dominique sneered, heading for the door with Olivier. The two went out.

Pierre pulled a chair over and Julien sat down, put his head back, and held a rag to his nose. It took almost ten minutes to stanch the bleeding. Once it had stopped for good, Julien asked Bastian to accompany him to the post office. Despite the butcher's advice to go home instead, Julien insisted he needed to finish up something urgent at work.

Julien actually had nothing to finish up, but being in his house summoned up too many bad memories of his youth. The internal wound inflicted by Dominique's words had hurt him more than the punch in the nose. After Bastian dropped him off at the post office, he closed the outer door and wandered around disconsolately before sitting down in the storeroom surrounded by boxes of mail. There he broke down and wept bitter tears of rage and impotence, not for Dominique, but for Bernadette. He found a box containing six bottles of wine, addressed to Monsieur Armand Boissieu. Disregarding this, he opened one and began to drink. After all, he thought, Armand belonged to a wine club and received a shipment like this every month, so he shouldn't be unduly upset to find one of his bottles missing.

By nine thirty that night, Julien was finishing up the second bottle. His eyelids felt like slabs of stone. The bell to the office began to ring insistently. Julien had no intention of opening the door for anyone, but the sound became so annoying that he finally decided to answer it just to make it stop. He stumbled to the door and discovered that the obstinate ringer was Father André.

Julien looked at his reflection in the glass of the door. His nose was the size and color of a purple lemon. When he attempted to touch it, the pain was unbearable, so he left it alone and opened the door.

"Good evening, Father André, do you need something?"

"I came to see how you were. Come on, let me in." The

priest entered and closed the door behind him. Julien went back to the storeroom and sat down next to the box of wine.

Father André continued. "Pierre told me what happened. This Dominique gets more unbearable by the day. He's obnoxious." He tried to get Julien to show him his nose. "That doesn't look good. It's going to be bruised for at least a couple of weeks."

The priest sat down next to the mailman. Seeing the open box of wine and the empty bottles, he said, "That's not the solution, Julien. You'll only hurt yourself more that way."

"No I won't," Julien said. "This wine is excellent."

The priest looked more closely at the bottle and raised his eyebrows. "But my son, you're drinking a special vintage of Château Margaux! No wonder it's excellent. Are you aware of what this wine costs? The owner isn't going to be happy at all when he finds out."

"Don't worry, Father, this happens all the time at the post office." Julien reached out and peeled a label off the box. "See this label?" He tore it up. "This package just got lost in the mail. The insurance will cover it and they'll send another box to Armand."

"It's that easy?" Father André asked, surprised.

"No problem," Julien said, reaching for another bottle. He opened it and asked, "Would you like to try it, Father André?"

"Well, I guess I could, just to keep you company. If the package is lost, after all, we shouldn't waste it."

"Very good," Julien said, swallowing in an attempt to stave off the attack of hiccups he'd felt coming on for a while. "You'll find two glasses on that shelf."

The priest got up and brought the glasses. Julien filled them to the brim and the two men toasted and drank.

"This wine is superb," said the priest.

"I told you it was, Father."

"Now tell me what's upsetting you. It was only a brawl, and you got a fist in the face that wasn't intended for you."

"First let's toast again." They clinked their glasses and emptied them. Julien refilled them again. "It wasn't the punch," he admitted. "What gets me is that Dominique doesn't realize how lucky he is to be with a woman like Bernadette, and the worst part is that she doesn't realize what kind of man she's married to. He cheats on her, did you know?"

"Don't let it upset you, Julien. What goes around comes around. Bernadette is a good woman and if you care for her you should want what's best for her."

"And I do, Father." They drank again. "What I can't stand is how that brute makes her suffer."

"Relax. Everything will work out. Let's enjoy this outstanding wine!" He lifted his glass and looked at Julien. "Let's toast to love!"

They clinked glasses again, and not for the last time. An hour later, two more bottles were empty and they were singing old songs from their student days, their arms slung around each other's shoulders. Julien picked a letter out of one of the boxes and tore it open. "Let's see who's writing the mayor." He began to read.

Dear Mr. Lefebvre,

We regret to inform you that your son Florian has again been absent from his courses this semester. If he continues this behavior, he will be barred from obtaining the title of Agricultural Technician offered by this vocational college.

"So Florian isn't studying engineering!" Father André broke in. "After all the bragging his father does about him, it turns out he's in vocational school. I think I'll have to recommend that the mayor come to confession."

"I propose a toast to Florian," Julien said, raising his glass. "The agricultural non-expert."

The two clinked their glasses together and drank. The priest stretched out his arm and chose another letter from the box.

"My turn." He glanced at the address and opened the envelope. "It's a letter for Brigitte, the sister of the nose-buster."

"I'm not making a toast to that," said Julien, gingerly touching his nose.

"That girl has problems," Father André answered, and began reading out loud:

Dear Brigitte,

Thank you very much for registering for our correspondence course, "Depilating the pubic area."

"I'll drink to that!" Julien raised his glass again. "To the depilation of the pubic area."

They toasted and raised their glasses. As Julien drank, the priest said, "I can state with authority that that girl doesn't need any further instruction on pubic hair removal."

"There's no way *you* can state that with authority!" Julien poured more wine. "Let's have another glass."

They drank again, and Julien picked a letter. "My turn. Let's see: *Monsieur Philippe Chardin*. This one's for Sergeant Chardin."

"Good man! Yes sir. Let's drink to him," Father André cheered. They raised their glasses and drank, after which Julien opened the letter.

Dear Philippe,

Last month I was vacationing in Madeira, spending a few days with my family, and I found some specimens of Danaus Plexippus. Since I already have several, I thought you might like one. I've enclosed it here.

I hope you enjoy it.

A warm hug from your friend Maxim.

The priest and the mailman looked at each other, mystified. Julien picked up the envelope from the floor and looked inside, then put his hand in and pulled something soft out of the envelope. It was a dead butterfly swarming with tiny ants that ran up Julien's arm. The mailman jumped up and shook his hand over and over, trying to rid himself of the creatures while the priest watched, glass in hand and a deadpan expression on his face.

"How disgusting! What kind of person sends dead bugs in an envelope?" Julien continued to give little hops as he rubbed his hands on his pants.

"I didn't know Chardin was a fan of butterflies," murmured Father André from the floor. "It's hard to imagine those fat fingers handling something so small." He pantomimed impaling a butterfly on a pin.

Finally Julien resumed his seat and the priest poured the remainder of the bottle into his glass. The two men looked at each other and began to laugh.

"You realize people are not what they seem," Father André said, draping his arm over Julien's shoulders. "We've all got our secrets, our yearnings. That's a good thing. Don't think everyone else is happy and you're the only exception. You'll see, life has some good surprises in store for you. You just have to be there to receive them when they come."

Julien nodded and patted the priest's leg. He got up. "Let's go, Father André, it's time to go home." He helped the other man to his feet. "I think I should walk you home."

The street was deserted when they left the post office. The night was serene and the full moon illuminated the road ahead of them. They filled their lungs with the fresh, cool air. As they walked toward the church, they both observed that the bell tower looked more beautiful than ever. Without knowing exactly why, each felt very fortunate to live in Sainte Marie.

23

August 24

Julian brushed his lips over Bernadette's back, pausing every few inches to deposit a kiss. For the mailman, getting to kiss the back of his beloved was like an endless dream that had finally come true. Each time he withdrew his lips from Bernadette's skin, he quivered as if she might suddenly disappear, and each time he pressed them to her again, a feeling of overwhelming peace pervaded him. When he reached the nape of her neck, he buried his nose in her hair and allowed her aroma to flood through him, transporting him twenty years into the past. He caressed her naked shoulders toasted by the summer sun and ran his hands down her arms until her hands clasped his like two final pieces of a puzzle falling into place. The lovers lay together resting on the white sheets, he holding her from behind and she resting her head on his arm. They watched the rain fall through the window and felt complete.

"I can't stop caressing you," murmured Julien, kissing the nape of her neck.

"You're tickling me!" she answered happily.

"I feel as if the last twenty years of my life have been nothing but a parenthesis, and that it's really only been a week since that St. John celebration."

"I was so stupid. I don't know how I let Dominique convince me. I was—"

"Don't think about that any more," Julien interrupted her.

"No." She turned toward him, her face scant inches from his. "I was so angry to think you'd been cheating on me that I couldn't even think straight. I loved you, and I wanted you to love me—but he was so convincing."

"Don't focus on the past. We have the rest of our lives ahead of us."

"I love you so much!" She embraced him. They kissed for a few minutes and then Bernadette laid her head on Julien's chest.

"What do we do now?" she asked. "How do we tell Dominique?"

"I'll tell him. He'll have to understand. If necessary, we'll leave Sainte Marie."

"And what about my children?"

"They'll come with us. I'll love them as if they were my own."

"They actually never spend any time with their father," Bernadette said, playing with Julien's chest hair. "Knowing Dominique, he'll be thrilled not to have to put up with them every day."

"Of course. Everything will turn out just fine."

"Where have you been all these years?" Bernadette lifted

her head and kissed him again.

"Delivering your mail."

They both laughed from the sheer happiness of being together.

"Where was Dominique off to in such a hurry anyway, and in the middle of this storm?"

"He's still obsessed with the lottery. He thinks the winner's going to be leaving town today to cash in his ticket. Dominique called his lowlife friends and told them to stand guard and not let the winner leave. It's just another excuse to go partying."

"He's insane, he's lost his mind. He doesn't realize this affair is out of his hands. I hope he doesn't do something stupid."

"You don't know who won, do you, Julien?" Bernadette asked, looking into his eyes.

"I'll tell you a secret." He sat up and leaned against the headboard. "I play every week, and I always pick different numbers. That week I played, but I didn't look at the ticket. When I found out there had been a winner, I know you're going to say I'm crazy, but I didn't want to check the numbers on my ticket. I waited to see if the winner would come forward. I thought he would do it right away. I told myself, if no one shows up with the winning ticket, that will mean I won."

"And how could you keep from looking at the number? I wouldn't have been able to restrain myself."

"The life of a mailman isn't that exciting, you know?"

"So . . . ?" Bernadette was impatient.

"At first it was like a game. As the days went by and the winner didn't reveal himself, I would daydream about what I would spend all that money on. Of course you were always in those dreams. They were all just variations on the theme of you and me together somewhere in the world."

"And then?"

"Well, then, things started to happen in the village. Your husband became obsessed, people started to suspect each other, the atmosphere got really tense. What had been a dream at first turned into a nightmare. I got frightened and hoped my number wasn't the winning one after all. I even thought of destroying the ticket without looking at it."

"You wouldn't!"

"No." He smiled. "After all, you don't see 152 million euros every day."

"So did you win?" asked Bernadette, excited.

"I'm sorry to disappoint you, but when I finally looked at the numbers I hadn't gotten even one right."

"You're so silly," she said affectionately and kissed him. "For a moment I thought it was you."

"Imagine what *I* thought. The winner was nowhere to be seen and I had a ticket I still hadn't looked at. Logically, I thought I must have the winning ticket."

"I wish!"

"Believe me, it's better this way. The day Dominique hit me I went to check my ticket, intending to cash it in and leave town forever. If I had, this would never have happened!" They both laughed.

"But why would you leave town? Everyone here loves you. It was only a punch in the nose, and you can't even see it any more."

"The punch didn't hurt as much as what he said to me. He made me believe you were too good for me and that I could never have been with you."

"Now you see that isn't true." Bernadette kissed him passionately. "What made you change your mind and come here today?" she asked.

"There are times in life when you have to make decisions, and I decided this was the right moment for me."

"Twenty years later? You certainly took your time deciding—though you did end up choosing the right moment."

"I guess it was just luck . . . with a little help from the church." He smiled.

"That Father André is so indiscreet! He's terrible. The confidentiality of the confessional means nothing to him. When his superiors find out—" They both laughed again.

"Don't get upset, the man only does it to help. Or would you rather he'd held his tongue?"

"You're right. He acts more like a matchmaker than a priest."

A light came through the window. This time it wasn't a bolt of lightning, it was headlights. It took Julien and Bernadette a few seconds to react.

"Oh my God, it's Dominique!" Bernadette said, terrified.

"Don't worry. I'll handle him," Julien said soothingly as they rushed to pull on their clothes.

"Are you sure? I'm ready for whatever happens. I love you and I don't think I could bear to lose you again."

"Hush. Nothing's going to change what happened here today. You and I are going to be together forever. But right now I think it's better for you not to be here. Go out the terrace door so he doesn't see you."

Still half-naked, they scurried down the hall, quickly buttoning up their clothes.

"Okay." Julien gave her what he hoped wouldn't be their last kiss. "I love you."

"I love you too."

The doorbell rang. *That's odd*, thought Bernadette. Maybe her husband had forgotten his keys? She finished dressing and walked toward the door, looking out the window in passing. The car parked in front of the house wasn't hers. Bernadette turned and motioned for Julien to wait a moment. He ducked into the kitchen and stood without moving a muscle, hoping to overhear the conversation. The rain was too noisy, though, so he peeked between the hinges of the kitchen door. The bell rang again and from outside came a deep voice.

"Bernadette! Please open the door. I'm François, the mayor, and I need your help."

24

August 1

As he walked through the door of Pierre's bar, Jean Baptiste fished a blue bandanna from his pants pocket, shook it out, and ran it over his neck to dry the sweat. He took off the straw hat he used to protect himself from the sun, revealing hair that was glued to his head. Drops of perspiration ran down the scruff of his neck and onto his back, wetting the salmon-colored shirt he wore. By this point in the summer, the sun was merciless. Each day seemed hotter than the one before, but that didn't keep Jean Baptiste from fulfilling his duties. High summer was actually his busiest time; there were periods when he watered around the clock. He took advantage of irrigating the largest estates to take catnaps next to the canals. On this particular day he'd already worked more than thirty hours straight. He wanted an ice-cold beer, after which he planned to go home and sleep.

"Good morning, all," he said as he entered.

Several customers interrupted the lively conversation going back and forth between the tables and the bar to return his greeting. Jean Baptiste walked up to the bar where Pierre was filling a plate with olives.

"Good morning, Pierre," said Jean Baptiste. "I can't believe how crowded it is in here."

"Good morning, Jean Baptiste. It's the time of day. People always come in for a quick drink before going home to eat. What can I get you?"

"I'll have a small draft beer." He set a ring of keys to the estates he watered on the bar. "Ice-cold, Pierre."

"One beer coming up, and some almonds to go with it, courtesy of the house, of course."

"I wouldn't expect anything less here, thanks." He took a sip, reveling in the icy coldness. "I'm trashed, Pierre. I've been watering without a break since six yesterday morning. It's so hot everyone wants their place watered. Let's see if we get a little rain."

"I don't think we're going to get a break on the weather until the end of September."

"Not necessarily. It's rained so little this year, maybe the rains will come early and we'll get a nice storm at the end of August." He lowered his voice and added, "It's because of global warming, you know."

"Yeah, of course." Pierre had heard of climate change, but had never thought it would reach Sainte Marie d'Azur.

Jean Baptiste enjoyed his beer while Pierre attended to his other customers. He was delighted to have so many; surely this would be a good summer. All at once the satisfaction on his face turned to worry when he saw Dominique come through the door for the first time since the fight with Bastian. The baker was alone this time. He approached the bar, his face set, and sat down to the left of Jean Baptiste. Pierre came over, unsmiling.

"Give me a beer, Pierre," said Dominique.

"I hope you're not planning to start any trouble. We've had enough problems lately."

"All I want is to drink a beer in peace. Are you going to give me one or not?"

Pierre set a glass in front of him and opened a small bottle of beer. Still without smiling, he said, "Here you are."

Dominique's only answer was a sneer. He poured the beer into his glass and began to drink while Pierre resumed his conversation with the irrigator.

"Tell me, Jean Baptiste, how's the fig production this year?"

"It hasn't been this good for years, though it varies from place to place. For example, the mayor's orchard is bursting with fruit. Others not so much, but overall much better than last year."

"The other day people were talking about installing drip irrigation systems," Pierre commented.

"That won't work here—you still end up using the same amount of water," the irrigator hastened to reply. "The only one making any money on that's the company that installs it. The trees need to be flooded with water for the fruit to develop properly."

"I think there's a conflict of interest here," Pierre teased. "You just don't want people installing drip systems and making you obsolete."

"Well, there's that too," answered Jean Baptiste with a smile. His cell phone began to ring. After a short conversation, he hung up and drained his beer. "How much do I owe you, Pierre? I've got to go."

"Has something happened?" Pierre asked.

"Nothing important, but it's going to keep me away from my bed a while longer. The mayor wants me to go open the gates to the countess's estate for an appraiser. Looks like he's been wanting to buy it for a couple of months now."

At this, Dominique sat up straight in his chair. *Could the mayor be the winner of the lottery? There's no other explanation,* he thought. The estate belonging to the countess was the largest in the area. The mayor wasn't strapped for cash, but buying an estate of that size was quite another kettle of fish. Besides, if he'd been thinking about it for a couple of months now, that would fit with the dates for the lottery prize. *He sure has kept it hushed up!* thought the baker. *He'll close on it at a good price before the countess knows he's the winner.*

"You have a good day, Pierre," said Jean Baptiste, leaving the bar.

"You do the same, and don't work too hard," Pierre called after the irrigator.

Once Jean Baptiste had left, Dominique moved closer to Pierre.

"Another beer, Dominique?"

"No. Listen," he said, leaning over the bar toward Pierre. "Did you hear what Jean Baptiste said about the mayor?"

"Yes, so?"

"Doesn't it seem strange to you that the mayor wants to buy the countess's property?"

Pierre looked at him in guarded bafflement.

"How much is that estate worth, Pierre? At least three or four million euros, right?" Pierre nodded. "And that's without counting the mansion on it."

"Okay . . . So what are you trying to tell me?" Pierre was completely lost.

"I don't think the mayor has the money to buy that estate," Dominique said with a meaningful look at Pierre, hoping he would finally get it.

"So why does he want to look at it if he can't buy it?"

"Maybe he can buy it now. Pierre, does the mayor play the lottery?"

"Of course, he has since the first day we opened."

"Well, the only other explanation is that the mayor's the winner."

This idea left Pierre speechless. Could it be true? The winner hadn't come forward, after all, and if the mayor was interested in buying the estate, maybe the only way he could do it was with the money from the lottery. "It's a disgrace for a man like him to have kept it quiet all this time, especially with everything that's happened in the village as a result of the winner not showing himself," Pierre said.

"You see? These things always happen with the people you least expect," Dominique said, adding, "You know what I think? That the mayor's plan is to quietly take over the whole village without saying a word. How long has he had this perverse obsession about being in charge of everything in Sainte Marie d'Azur? Now he's trying to become some sort of king. The worst thing is that if he'd admitted to being the winner, our village would now be full of tourists and investors. You and I would be making money off all those people. The whole village would have prospered."

Pierre listened closely to Dominique's harangue.

"And I'll tell you something else, Pierre. The mayor is robbing us of future income. It's what they call 'the opportunity cost.'"

"Of course, the opportunity cost." It seemed to Pierre that he'd heard that term on some radio program.

"If we'd known who the winner was since the day after the winning number was announced, you would be thinking about expanding your business now. Doesn't it come as a surprise to you that after having sold the ticket that won the largest prize of the EuroMillions right here at this lottery retailer, people aren't lining up around the block to buy here? The 'luckiest village in Europe' has turned into the unluckiest because the winner hasn't come forward. People don't believe it until the happy winner appears on TV saying he was the lucky one."

"You're right. It's shameful what M. François has done to us. We should talk to him and tell him just what we think of his behavior. And to think I've always voted for him."

The bar's other customers had begun to gather around Pierre and Dominique. One neighbor added, "I've always voted for him too, since the very first time he ran, but there's no way I'll vote for him after this. What a nerve!"

"We need to read him the riot act!" said another customer.

"It would have been so easy for him to say he was the winner from the very first day." Dominique continued his harangue. "The reason he didn't is that he's trying to take over the town little by little. I wouldn't be surprised to hear he'd been asking about more land to buy up."

The bar was abuzz with speculation. At least fifteen patrons were discussing the subject. The evidence was conclusive; if the mayor was going to buy the countess's estate, it was with the money from the lottery. The customers were getting more incensed by the minute. For the good of everyone in the village, the mayor should admit he was the winner, to keep the village from utter collapse. If he didn't do it voluntarily, they would force him to. One man proposed going to the town hall and making him confess, and the rest applauded the initiative. All the patrons set out in a posse headed for the government building. People they passed in the street joined them after hearing their complaint.

The group reached the government building and trooped up the wooden staircase to the second floor where the mayor's office was. Amélie, his administrative assistant, attempted to bar their access to the outer office, but there were too many people. At the door to the mayor's office, Pierre addressed his secretary. "Good morning, Cecile, we'd like to see M. François."

"He's not in his office at the moment," said the secretary, a bit intimidated at seeing such a crowd.

"You can't stop us! We're the citizens of this town and we want to see our mayor!" someone shouted from the back of the group.

"Let's go in!" yelled another.

The crowd shoved Pierre forward. Frightened, Cécile ducked out of their way and called Sergeant Chardin from her desk phone, imploring him to come immediately to the town hall.

The mob pushed their way into the office, which, as the secretary had indicated, was empty. A few of the townspeople took advantage of being in the mayor's office to sit in his chair and put their feet up on his paper-strewn desk. Dominique left the office and found Cécile.

"Where is the mayor?"

"He's in the meeting room. There's a city council meeting today," said the secretary.

"Friends! To the meeting room! That's where M. François is!" shouted the baker.

One by one, the horde abandoned the office and headed to the meeting room on the first floor. Reaching the door, they threw it open and pushed inside.

"What's this all about?" shouted M. François indignantly. "You're interrupting a plenary session! This is an outrage!"

The mayor's tone cowed some members of the rowdy crowd, who hung their heads. "Would you mind explaining what's going on here?" insisted M. François when no one spoke.

"That's what we'd like to know!" yelled someone from the back. This emboldened the rest of the mob and everyone began to shout.

"Tell the truth!"

"The village belongs to all, not just one!"

"We refuse to become your employees!"

"Down with M. François!"

The mayor didn't have the faintest idea of what was happening. The anxious councilmen tried to find out from some of the townspeople what had happened. In the midst of the uproar, one town councilman approached M. François. "They're saying you won the lottery. Is it true?"

"What do you mean, I won the lottery? Don't talk nonsense."

"These people are angry because they think you're going to buy up all the village lands."

"What foolishness is this!?" said M. François.

He got up from his chair and waved his arms in the air to quiet the crowd. When the hubbub died down, he said, "One at a time." When several began to talk, he shouted, "Just one!"

The crowd urged Pierre to talk. Though he was not at all anxious to be the spokesperson for the mob, the stern looks of his companions convinced him to speak. "Mr. Mayor," he began, swallowing. "We've learned that you may possibly be the winner of the lottery, and we think you've been very unfair to the people of this village by keeping it secret all this time."

"Where did you get such a ridiculous idea, Pierre?" asked M. François.

"Isn't it true you're going to buy the countess's property?" asked someone the mayor couldn't identify.

"We know you're going to buy it," said Pierre. "We don't want you to buy up all the village land. Besides, there's the opportunity cost, and that's a lot of money."

"What's that you're saying about the opportunity cost of what?" M. François was completely in the dark about whatever the hell Pierre was talking about.

"You know," answered Pierre. "The opportunity cost. The opportunity to make more money that we haven't had."

"Let's move on." M. François still didn't understand what Pierre meant.

"Is it true you're planning to buy the countess's property

or not?" asked Dominique.

"Yes and no," said the mayor.

To most of the crowd, this answer was as good as a confession. There were immediate shouts for the mayor to resign, and a number of people began to chant, "The people, united, will never be defeated."

"One moment!" M. François tried once again to restore silence. "One moment, please!"

Little by little, the noise died down and the mayor continued. "It's true I'm going to buy the countess's estate, or better said, all of us are going to buy it." The faces of the mob filled with bewilderment. "I've never won anything from the lottery, much less this prize. The town government has been negotiating with the countess for months now to purchase a part of her land with the goal of building a modern sports complex for Sainte Marie."

This was met with utter silence.

"The town councilmen present here today can corroborate what I just told you. We haven't wanted to make it public yet in order to avoid speculators coming in and driving up the price. It's complicated enough already to obtain the credit we need to buy the part we're looking at."

"So then it's not true you won the lottery?" one of the women asked.

"Of course not. I know we're all on edge because the winner hasn't come forward, but we mustn't lose our heads."

Accompanied by two police officers, Sergeant Chardin chose this moment to make his way through the crowd.

"Are you all right, Mr. Mayor?" he asked when he reached

him.

"Don't worry, Chardin, everything's under control," M. François answered, turning to the crowd. "These townspeople are just leaving, aren't you?"

Hanging their heads, the people turned to go. Some, aware of having lost their heads, regretted having expressed their fears about the lottery in such a public way. The truth was that the amount of time that had gone by without the winner making himself known had begun to take its toll on the morale of the village.

That week, Father André delivered the most severe sermon anyone in Sainte Marie could remember. He accused the townspeople collectively of having become avaricious beings who sought only to amass earthly riches when there was no need. According to the priest, the villagers had sunk to a new low, where they wished misfortune on each other in an attempt to make themselves feel better. He told them he would pray for mercy on their souls. The priest's words resonated in the minds of many long afterwards.

"Originally a stroke of good luck, the lottery prize has become for us the eleventh biblical plague. If we're unable to return to the days when harmony reigned in this village and you all loved each other, it will be the end of us. Reflect on what each of you has done these past weeks and the thoughts you've harbored about each other. I know your consciences are not at rest. Reflect on that."

From that day forth, the lottery was not mentioned again in the village. People were genuinely ashamed of their attitudes. Dominique tried to bring the topic up again several times, but no one wanted to talk about it. Only Olivier followed Dominique's lead though truth be told, the affair had begun to bore him as well. The village residents seemed unable to recover their former good cheer. When they met on the street, their comments were limited to brief greetings and people hid themselves away in their houses at night, reluctant to fraternize. Pierre's bar became deserted, its only patrons the tourists who passed through Sainte Marie on bus tours. The number of people who got together for a drink before lunch dwindled.

In little more than three months, the luckiest village in Europe had become the saddest.

25

August 24

The storm had hidden the sun for hours now and when the eight o'clock service began, it looked as if night had already fallen. Ever since the advent of daylight savings time in spring, every Mass Father André had celebrated had been during daylight hours. He'd hoped not to have to turn on the lights in the church until the summer was over, but tonight it was necessary.

While the priest officiated, Adrien, Jeanette, and Charlie listened from their seats in the second pew on the right. The storm had kept everyone else away and Adrien had attempted to convince Father André to forgo giving Mass, but the priest had said, "Mass must be celebrated even though no one is present. You never know. Besides, you three are here, and you will surely benefit from it."

Hearing this, Adrien had decided to give up, a decision further strengthened by his wife stepping on his foot.

"For Yours is the kingdom and the power and the glory forever," intoned the priest, adding, "May the peace of the Lord be with you."

"And with your spirit," answered Jeanette, elbowing Adrien to respond with her.

"Let us offer each other a sign of peace," concluded Father André.

Jeanette and Adrien gave each other a kiss on the cheek and kissed Charlie. The little boy enthusiastically ran to the altar to offer a kiss to the priest. Taken by surprise, Father André graciously accepted it before continuing with the Mass. Instead of returning to his seat, Charlie wandered off into one of the side aisles of the church. His father got up to look for him, but Jeanette pulled him back down.

"Leave him alone, Mass is almost over." She turned toward where Charlie was playing and looked back at Adrien. "He won't move from there."

What was really bothering Adrien wasn't Charlie. Going to look for his son had been an excuse to get up from that pew. Being in the empty church was beginning to weigh on him. For her part, Jeanette just wanted Mass to be over quickly. She hoped Adrien and Charlie would behave themselves until it was finished and not do anything to disrupt it and make a bad impression on Father André, who had been so kind to them all afternoon. Both she and Adrien were aware that they might have to stay overnight in the village. The storm showed no signs of letting up, and no sane person would dare get on the highway under those conditions. If they hadn't stopped at the church, they would have arrived at their hotel hours ago, a thought that would at any other time have put them into a very bad mood—but today they'd really enjoyed Father André's company. And after all, they were on vacation.

After receiving Communion, the couple knelt for a few moments. Adrien raised his eyes a couple of times to check on Charlie. The little boy was contemplating the image of a saint with an axe in its hand. Adrien smiled for a second.

Though Charlie looked brave now, he would no doubt have nightmares tonight about the saint with the axe.

Suddenly the church went dark. The only light was a faint intermittent glow outside the windows when the sun peeked through the storm clouds. Terrified, Charlie began to scream, "Mommy! Mommy!"

Jeanette tried to calm him. "Stay where you are, Charlie. I'll be right there!"

Father André's voice sounded from the darkness. "Relax, my children, don't be afraid. I'm sure the light will come back on quickly. This happens frequently when there's a cold front coming in."

Keeping his hand on the back of one of the pews, Adrien felt his way toward the place he'd last seen Charlie. "Charlie, are you there?" His voice came out in a whisper, which momentarily surprised him. Reality quickly reasserted itself, though, and he realized speaking in a low voice out of respect for where they were didn't make much sense under the circumstances. More energetically, he called, "Charlie, say something so I know where you are!"

"I'm here, Daddy."

The childish voice seemed to come from only a few yards away. Unfortunately, Adrien had come to the end of the pew and had to venture forth blindly in an unfamiliar church full of invisible obstacles. Summoning up his fatherly valor, he took a step and then another. It seemed easier that he had thought it would be.

Crash!

Adrien had blundered into some unidentifiable object that fell to the floor, making a tremendous racket. The ringing of coins rolling over the floor tiles could be heard. Father André came out from behind the altar carrying a flashlight.

"Stay calm, everything's fine! Are you all okay?" asked the priest.

Adrien and Jeanette answered that they were. Charlie said in a small voice, "Daddy did it."

Just then the lights came back on, making the church interior seem much brighter than it had before. Adrien squeezed his eyes shut, and then tried to open them, but a nearby bulb shone directly into his face, blinding him. He felt a sharp pain in his eyes and half-closed them again, not before glimpsing his son a few feet away behind the saint with the axe. Adrien groped his way toward him. His eyes adjusted quickly and when he reached Charlie he saw what he'd run into. It was a votive stand that held candles and a box for offerings to the saints. The box had fallen off the stand and broken open when it hit the floor, spilling a few coins onto the tile.

"Everything seems to be in order," said Father André, coming toward Adrien. "Let's light a few candles in case it happens again."

"I'm very sorry I bumped into this. I should have stayed where I was, but I heard Charlie and had to find him," Adrien apologized.

"Don't worry, my son," Father André said, righting the votive stand. "The important thing is we're all all right, no?"

"You're so good, Father," said Jeanette. She knelt down and began to pick up the candles from the floor. "Let us help you put this back together. We'll pay for any damage, of course."

"Don't be silly, my daughter. Nothing has happened here that an old priest can't fix with a bit of wire."

"Adrien can fix it for you right now. He's very handy," said Jeanette. "Right, Adrien?"

"Of course, Father, no problem," answered her husband, who had already picked up the votive stand. "Where should I put this?"

"There, next to Saint Jude." The priest realized Adrien didn't know which saint he was referring to and added, "The one with the axe."

Adrien carried the stand to the image and set it down carefully. Jeanette followed and began to tuck the candles away in their place.

"I didn't know Saint Jude carried an axe," remarked Jeanette.

"Saint Jude was killed by having his head cut off with an axe. That's why some images portray him holding an axe. Not very many, though; this is one of the few in France," said Father André.

"Oh, of course," said Adrien. "They cut off his head because he betrayed Christ."

"Many people think that, but the one who betrayed Jesus was actually Judas Iscariot, not Jude the Apostle. This one is the patron saint of impossible causes." Father André realized Adrien must feel like a fool and quickly added, "Don't worry, my son, lots of people confuse them. Saint Jude doesn't have many devotees in France compared to Germany, Italy, and most of all, America. Here he's a saint without many followers. The tourists prefer the statue of Saint John, which is one of the oldest in Europe. It was buried in a ditch for ages to keep it from being stolen or destroyed. Finally it was unearthed and restored, and now lots of tourists come to see it. As you see, Saint John and Bastian the butcher's special sausages are our village's chief attractions."

The money box that had fallen from the votive stand was lying on the floor under the image of the saint. When Jeanette saw it, she kneeled and began to gather up the coins that had rolled from it, all small change. Father André bent over to help her.

"You see, I'm not lying," he said. "Normally no one leaves anything for poor Saint Jude. Look how few coins there are, and I haven't checked the box for months. In contrast, not a week goes by that the one containing the offerings to Saint John isn't overflowing."

"The box broke," Jeanette said regretfully, picking it up from the floor. She opened it to replace the small handful of coins she'd collected.

"Don't concern yourself, it can be fixed," Father André consoled her. He took the box to close it, glancing inside, then stopped. "What's this?" he said, putting his hand in and taking out a slip of paper.

"What is it, Father?" asked Jeanette.

"It can't be," he said, unfolding the piece of paper. "It's a lottery ticket!"

The priest stared at the ticket for a few seconds, his heart beating so hard he thought it would burst from his chest. Dropping the box with a crash that echoed through the church, he ran for the sacristy.

"Is something wrong, Father André?" Adrien shouted after him.

Jeanette looked at her husband and back at the door through which the priest had exited. "Is it possible?" she asked Adrien.

"Do you think that's the famous lottery ticket? It doesn't

make sense."

"I don't know, but I'm pretty sure that's what Father André thinks."

The priest appeared again, dashing through the same door, out of breath, a newspaper in his hand. At the statue of Saint Jude, he held out the newspaper and the lottery ticket to Jeanette. The paper, dated May 25th, was opened to the page listing the results of the various drawings. The opposite page trumpeted the headline *France Awards the Largest Prize in EuroMillions History*.

Jeanette compared the numbers on the ticket. They matched. In her hand she held 152 million euros. She let out a whoop of excitement and hugged Father André. Adrien grabbed the newspaper and the ticket out of her hands and compared the numbers for himself. "It's incredible!" he exclaimed while Jeanette and Father André danced around him. Without understanding the reason for the jubilation, Charlie joined in the dance.

"But can it still be redeemed?" Adrien's question stopped Jeanette and the priest in mid-spin.

"What time is it?" Jeanette asked her husband.

"8:45."

"What time does the lottery retailer here in the village close, Father? The one next to our house closes at nine, right?" she said, looking at Adrien.

"I think so," he answered.

"There's no separate lottery retailer here," said Father André. "Tickets are sold and redeemed in Pierre's bar."

"That will work," said Jeanette. "Where's the bar?"

"Ri—right across from the church," stuttered the priest, whose legs were shaking. "Shall we go?"

"Of course, Father! We have ten minutes to cash in this ticket!" Jeanette took it and tucked it safely into her pocket. "Which way?"

"Let's go out the main door; that's closest," said the priest. "But better let's take an umbrella so we don't get wet."

"Forget the umbrella, Father! We only have a few minutes left," Jeanette urged. "Better to redeem the ticket and get wet than risk arriving too late."

"You two go, I'll stay here with Charlie," Adrien said, looking at his wife. She nodded.

Father André and Jeanette rushed to the main door of the church. Outside, it was raining much harder than they had imagined. The priest pointed to the bar across the street, and the two ducked into the torrential downpour. After only four giant strides, Father André slipped and fell into the enormous puddle that had formed in the gutter at the side of the street. Jeanette pulled him quickly to his feet and they hurried on. The scene was truly ghastly, between the pitch-black, deserted street and the deafening noise of the downpour.

They finally made it across the street and saw a light on in the bar. Entering, they found Pierre mopping up the water that had come in through a partly open window. He looked up, surprised.

"Father André, just look at you! Why in the world are you out in this downpour?" he asked.

"How late can we validate a lottery ticket?" Jeanette asked.

"Until nine," Pierre said. "Why?"

"I need you to validate this number," she said.

"Impossible. You'll have to come back tomorrow," Pierre answered.

"Pierre, don't be ridiculous!" Father André approached him and grabbed his arm, forcing him to put down the mop. "We need you to do it now!"

"I'd be happy to do it for you, Father, but I can't," said Pierre. "The machine stopped working when the electricity went out. It takes twenty minutes to reboot and connect with the switchboard at the main lottery office. Even if it could be connected right now, it's seven minutes to nine. There's not enough time. Come back tomorrow and we'll have plenty of time to do it then."

"You don't understand, Pierre. It's now or never," urged Father André. "We found the 152 million ticket!"

Jeanette pulled it out of her pocket and showed it to Pierre, who took it and looked up at a poster with the winning number emblazoned on it and the words "Sold here" above. After comparing the two numbers, he stood as if hypnotized.

"What can we do, Pierre?" begged Father André.

"I don't know. Let me think." He flipped the switch on the lottery machine and the words "REBOOTING. PLEASE WAIT" appeared on the screen.

"What?" demanded Jeanette.

"It's impossible. We won't make it in time," said Pierre.

"So what do we do now?" asked Father André.

"There's only one other possibility." The priest and Jeanette stared at Pierre, willing him to continue. "A notary public can corroborate that the winning ticket has appeared and the owner wishes to redeem it before midnight."

The three of them stood silently for a few seconds, looking at each other.

"Where is the notary?" Jeanette asked.

"There's no notary here," Father André said.

"Then we're doomed," Jeanette lamented, sitting down on a chair.

"There's still one possibility," Pierre said.

"Well, come on, what is it?!" Father André urged.

"There's a notary that works in Cannes and spends his summers in a chalet about twenty minutes from here. If you can go there, I'm sure he'll be able to help you," explained Pierre.

"He's probably not there today," said Jeanette.

"It's our only hope—we have to try," answered the priest.

"I think he's there," said Pierre. "He went to the butcher shop today to pick up some chops he'd ordered from Bastian because he was having friends over for dinner. That's how I know he spends his summers there. Afterwards he stopped off at the bar and we chatted for a while."

Jeanette made up her mind. "Let's go, then!"

"Pierre, come with us—you're the only one who knows where he lives," added Father André.

"I don't have a car, though," said Pierre.

"It doesn't matter," Jeanette put in. "Let's go get mine and we'll pick you up at the door in five minutes."

"Okay, I'm going to close up the bar then." Seeing the lottery ticket had put Pierre's nerves on high alert too. After so many weeks of talking about nothing but the lottery, the ticket had become a sort of holy relic.

Jeanette and Father André went out. Before crossing the street to the church, the priest took her by the arm under the bar awning. "Jeanette, I don't know if we'll be able to make it out of town tonight."

"Don't worry, Father, I've driven in the rain lots of times. I'll go slowly, but we'll make it in time."

"There's something that worries me more than the rain."

Jeanette threw him a perplexed look. "What?"

"I know a group of people from the village were talking about stopping anyone who tried to leave town tonight to cash in the ticket. They may have abandoned their plan because of the rain, but we can't be sure."

"That's crazy!"

"I told you and Adrien that the last three months have been a nightmare here." Father André looked into Jeanette's eyes. "I could never forgive myself if you were hurt for the sake of money."

"We have to try, Father André," Jeanette answered. "Besides, it's not just the money. As you said, there's only one way this village is going to go back to being the way it was before, and that's by cashing in this ticket."

"Then, as Julius Caesar said, *alea iacta est*."

"The die is cast," repeated Jeanette.

Father André nodded with a half smile on his lips and the two plunged into the downpour and ran for the church. The evening was becoming an odyssey. Both of them knew that victory was within their grasp—if luck was on their side.

26

August 24

There was nothing but static on the radio in Dominique's car. Olivier punched all the buttons but couldn't find a single station.

"Just leave it, Olivier. The electricity must be out on the antenna," Dominique said without moving his gaze from the street.

"I want to know if the storm's going to go on much longer. I wanted to go to the beach tomorrow."

Preoccupied with other things, Dominique didn't answer. He knew the argument he'd had with Bernadette that afternoon wasn't just one more in a long line of arguments. He hadn't felt anything for her for a long time now and had thought of leaving her more than once, but restrained himself so as not to provide more fodder for the village gossips. Right now he was trying to remember word for word what he'd said to her during their fight; he feared he might have said too much. For years now he'd employed a strategy with Bernadette designed to make her feel obligated to stay with him. Many times he'd told her that if she left him, she would be alone. He'd used comments like this to undermine her self-confidence and convince her that her only options were either to stay with Dominique or live her life alone, and he'd been successful. Until this very afternoon, Bernadette had still thought she'd been dumped by Julien, and considered herself fortunate to be with the baker. She would have done anything for her husband. This was a comfortable position for Dominique: he enjoyed the advantages of having a wife at home who gave him no problems and demanded little of him, while at the same time he could party with his friends and continue his romantic flings without worrying about Bernadette finding out. But now the baker saw clearly that he might have destroyed that status quo with his words.

"I got it!" Olivier's exclamation tore him from his thoughts. A faint melody could be heard amid the overwhelming static.

"What station did you find? It's music. You're not going to find out anything about the storm there."

"It's one minute to nine. There's a news bulletin every hour on the hour." Olivier fiddled with the knobs in an attempt to fine-tune the station.

"Christ, it's really coming down," the baker said. He lowered his head a fraction and tried to get a glimpse of the sky through the windshield.

"Dominique, why are we sitting here in front of the post office and not on the road out of town?" Olivier asked, his eyes fixed on the radio.

"You already know Chardin will cause problems for us if he sees the four of us together."

"But we'd be more effective somewhere else, next to Thierry and Pamphile, in case they need us. No one comes by here."

"If they need us we can be there in an instant." Dominique looked out the window again, as if waiting for someone. "Besides, I want to keep an eye out for Julien. I've had the feeling for weeks now that he knows more than he's telling. I don't know where he is, but he always comes back to the post office. If I see him I want to talk to him."

"That wimp? No doubt he's at home hiding from the rain." Olivier laughed at his own wit while Dominique sat stone-faced.

The deejay announced the hour and played the station's theme music. This was followed by the news, which began with coverage of international conflicts and the economy. The newscaster then cut to a reporter at the Civil Protection Agency headquarters. Olivier turned up the volume and listened carefully.

"Reporting from Civil Protection headquarters, the thunderstorm that began this afternoon in the Cannes area has intensified, surpassing initial forecasts. Several places in the interior have had more than four inches of rainfall since six p.m., but the worst is yet to come. Sources from the National Institute of Meteorology have informed us that the intensity of the storm is not expected to diminish in the next few hours. The continued rainfall may cause serious flooding, given that the rivers and gullies are already at capacity. This type of weather event is unusual for this time of year; normally severe thunderstorms occur at the end of September or the beginning of October as a result of cold fronts moving in. The Civil Protection Agency recommends that citizens remain in their homes unless it is absolutely necessary for them to go out. We will continue to keep you informed during our upcoming news bulletins."

"Dominique, I don't think anyone's leaving town today," Olivier said, turning off the radio. "You heard him, we should go home in case it gets even worse."

"We're not moving from this spot until midnight or until the winner tries to leave town."

"If he doesn't show up soon, we won't have time to redeem the ticket." The lottery issue had lost its appeal for Olivier by this time. All he wanted was the protection of his own house in case flooding did occur.

"Look. I'm going to tell you something, Olivier." The baker shifted sideways in the driver's seat and fixed his eyes on his friend. "I don't care about cashing in that ticket, but I'm not going to let anyone else do it either."

Olivier looked at Dominique's face and didn't recognize his lifelong friend.

27

August 24

"You have to turn right there, after the bar," Pierre indicated to Jeanette from the back seat of the Toyota Corolla.

"Let me know when we get there because I can't see anything with this rain!" she answered nervously.

"Never fear, my children. Everything is going to work out," said Father André from the passenger seat. "This is a divine mission we're on—since the ticket appeared in the church."

Pierre was folded into the seat behind the priest. All Jeanette could see of him were his arms that signaled the way. The windshield wipers, even on high, were useless against the sheets of water that coursed down the windshield. Everyone relaxed a little once they'd turned onto the street leading out of the village, but their relief lasted only a few seconds: all at once the streetlights went dark. The electricity had gone out again. Jeanette slowed down, fearful of running into a parked car.

"The next street is the highway," Pierre encouraged her,

excited about leaving town.

Father André was less sanguine about reaching the highway successfully. He peered silently though the windows, on the alert for what he most feared, but as they crept along without encountering obstacles, he relaxed little by little. Maybe Dominique and his henchmen had given up on their mission and gone home.

"There's the highway, just up ahead, on the right," said Pierre.

"I told you we had to try it, Father!" Jeanette said enthusiastically, turning toward the priest.

"Look out!" shouted Father André suddenly. A human figure had appeared in the middle of the road ahead of them, wearing a garbage bag as a raincoat.

Jeanette jammed on the brakes and the car hydroplaned on the sheet of water, sliding out of control as she yanked the steering wheel back and forth in a desperate attempt to keep them on the road. Even as they slid toward him, the man in the middle of the street held his ground. When the car finally came to a halt scant feet from him, Father André threw open the door and got out, furious. The rain drenched him instantly as he strode toward the man.

"Are you crazy? We could have hit you!" he shouted, still unsure of whom he was talking to.

"Don't worry, we'd already seen you," said Thierry.

His use of "we" confused the priest until Thierry was joined by a shorter man, also wearing a garbage bag as a raincoat, who had been waiting on the sidewalk. Jeanette and Pierre got out of the car and waded over to them.

"We're here to inform you that the highway is

impassable," Thierry said, scrutinizing the occupants of the red Toyota. "There was a landslide on account of the rain and we're cut off."

"In both directions?" asked Pierre, perplexed.

"Yes. Apparently the storm has caused major devastation," Pamphile hastened to add. "You need to return to your homes at once. Tomorrow when the storm is over, the damages will be repaired."

At that very moment, a car drove by on the highway. They all turned to look at it.

"Didn't you just say the highway was closed?" asked Jeanette. "So where's that car coming from then?"

They all looked at Thierry, even Pamphile, who had no idea what to say and hoped his companion would be able to come up with something.

"Well," said Thierry. "I've told you you can't pass and that's final. I don't know what sort of urgent mission you're on that makes you have to leave Sainte Marie right now with these conditions."

Father André realized the men were suspicious of their motives. Before Jeanette could answer, he interrupted. "My children, this young lady is a tourist who was trapped in our village by the storm. Since she's not familiar with the area, Pierre and I have offered to accompany her someplace she can find a bus or train to take her to the capital."

"Yes." Seeing that the priest was running out of arguments—he was obviously unused to lying—Jeanette stepped in. "All my luggage is at my hotel in Cannes. I didn't bring anything with me. I came here on the bus this morning to see a little of the area and got caught by the storm. I'm a little frightened, and it would be a great relief to me to be able to get back to my hotel tonight."

"I'm afraid I can't allow you to leave the village, Miss," responded Thierry. "It's too dangerous. I advise you to look for shelter tonight and tomorrow you can leave with no trouble."

Pamphile took Thierry by the arm, interrupting him. "If you'll allow us, we're getting a call with an update on the highway conditions." The two walked away and got into their car. Meanwhile, Pierre, Jeanette, and Father André huddled together. In a low voice, the priest warned them, "I don't trust these men's intentions. You know them, don't you, Pierre?"

"Yes, they're Dominique's friends. A couple of lowlifes."

"Exactly," the priest went on. "We'd better not insist or we could have problems."

"But why don't they want to let us leave?" Jeanette asked.

"These people have been trying to find the winner of the lottery for weeks now," said the priest. "They're dangerous. I wouldn't be surprised if they were planning to find the winner and steal the ticket from him. I think it would be prudent to go back and look for another way out of town."

"All right." Jeanette could find nothing else to say.

"Those two are never on their own, Father," Pierre said. "No doubt Dominique's behind this."

"I know. That's why I just thought of an idea, but I need Jeanette's help."

"I'll do whatever you want, Father."

"Careful, they're coming back," Pierre cautioned.

The two men approached them, smiling. "We have good news. Apparently the highway will reopen at midnight," Thierry informed them. "I guess you're in luck after all, Miss. You'll be able to get out of town tonight after all. It's already quarter to ten—you'll just have to wait a couple more hours."

"Unless," Pamphile broke in, "there's some reason you need to leave before that time. If that's the case, if it's an emergency, we could call back to ask for permission for you to leave now."

These two have the IQ of a fish, thought Jeanette. Their trap was glaringly obvious—though, had Father André not explained it to her a few seconds before, her urgency to leave Sainte Marie might have landed her in it.

"That's wonderful news! You don't know how happy that makes me. I really was a little frightened by the situation," she answered, and added, "So we'll just come back a little later, right, Father?"

"Of course, daughter, don't worry. Right now we'll make some dinner for you and later Pierre and I will accompany you," said Father André with a smile.

"Not much business on a day like today, anyway," added Pierre.

"In that case, why don't you come back later? I imagine you'll be able to get through then. If you don't see us here, you'll know the highway has reopened," said Thierry.

"Very well, my sons. Thank you for everything and goodnight," said Father André, turning toward the car.

"Yes, goodbye! And try to stay dry," Jeanette said, walking back to the Corolla.

They climbed into the car and turned around. Thierry and

Pamphile waved goodbye. When the Corolla had reached the end of the street, they congratulated themselves.

"You were right. That was a good way to find out if they wanted to leave town before midnight to redeem the ticket."

"I told you so! Do you think we should tell Dominique? He told us to keep him informed of anything that happened."

"I don't think it's necessary. They didn't leave, after all, and I've never seen the girl around here. I think it's obvious they were telling the truth. If they had had the lottery ticket, they wouldn't have been willing to wait until after midnight— they would have insisted on going now."

"You're right. That trick about waiting until after midnight worked."

As they continued to congratulate each other on the brilliance of their ruse, it dawned on them that they were standing in the middle of the street with the rain pouring down on them. They decided to take refuge in the car.

28

"Do you understand, Jeanette?" asked Father André.

"I think so, but I still don't get why you or Pierre can't just do it directly."

"Look, the mayor wants all this to be over. If he knows someone from the village has the winning ticket, he won't do anything to help if that means turning one of his other voters against him. He knows no one from this village deserves his help if they've kept the ticket secret all this time and are just trying to redeem it now at the last minute. I've told you everything that's happened because the winner didn't come forward. On the other hand, if it's someone from outside Sainte Marie, that's a different story. M. François doesn't want our village to look bad. If an outsider has the ticket and people from the village are keeping him from cashing it in, that would be a disgrace for him. That's what will get him to react and help us."

Pierre nodded. He couldn't agree more with the priest.

"All right, Father. If you're that convinced, we'll do it your way," Jeanette answered, adding, "Now pray for it to work!"

Father André picked up the receiver and dialed the mayor's home number. It was slightly after ten thirty, and the priest knew M. François was probably asleep, but time was short. He passed the phone to Jeanette, who listened to the rings and hoped someone would pick up.

"Yes?" Jeanette heard a hoarse voice at the other end of the line. Father André dipped his head at her, urging her to speak.

"Good evening," Jeanette said, her nerves accelerating her speech. "You don't know me—I'm not from Sainte Marie— but I'm in urgent need of your help. It's extremely important for you and everyone in your village."

"Please slow down, I can't understand you," M. François interrupted, trying to wake up.

Jeanette made a conscious effort to speak more slowly. "Yes, Mr. Mayor. My name is Jeanette. I'm not from Sainte Marie d'Azur. I have the winning ticket from the lottery three months ago, but I need your help to redeem it."

"What's that you say? You've got the lottery ticket?"

"Yes, Mr. Mayor. It's a long story, but for now I'll just say that we found the ticket this afternoon in the church and we're trying to leave town so we can redeem it. For the good of your village, you need to help us!"

"Who else is with you? What do you mean when you say 'we're trying to leave town'?"

"I'm at the church with Father André. He invited my husband and me to take refuge here when it started raining so hard. By pure chance we found the ticket in the church, but when we tried to leave the village, some people stopped us. We're calling to ask if you could call the headquarters of the Gendarmerie and request that they send a couple of patrol cars to the village. That way we'll be able to leave and find the notary public so he can certify that we showed him the ticket before twelve midnight."

"Listen, Miss, I don't understand any of this. Please be good enough to pass the phone to Father André to see if he can clarify this affair."

"He wants to talk to you." Jeanette passed the receiver to the priest.

"Good evening, François," said Father André.

"Can you clarify this for me? First of all, is it true the ticket's been found?"

"Absolutely. Someone put it into the offering box for Saint Jude. Incredible but true."

"That's amazing."

"The problem is that we've tried to redeem it, but since the electricity's going on and off, the machine in Pierre's bar won't work. So then we tried to leave the village and drive to the house of a notary public who lives nearby, but a couple of people stopped us. I suspect they're from Dominique's gang. The only solution is for you to call the Gendarmerie so they can send someone to protect us."

"That's not going to be possible."

"Why not?"

"Haven't you seen how it's coming down? Every member of the Gendarmerie is busy with the problems caused by the storm. I already called them about the possibility of sending us someone in case there was trouble with Dominique's gang, but the commander himself told me that all his officers have their hands full with the storm and he won't be able to spare anyone until the weather clears."

Father André was at a loss for words. Where could they go from there? His hopes for redeeming the ticket were dashed.

"I just thought of something, but it may be a stupid idea."

"Any idea is welcome right now. What are you thinking, François?"

"If Dominique's behind all this, maybe we can convince him to let us leave the village to redeem the ticket."

"I don't think that will work."

"I don't either, but Bernadette could convince him."

"Excellent idea!" exclaimed Father André with enthusiasm. "If we take Bernadette with us, he'll have to let us leave without any problems."

"She lives close to my house. I can go by and pick her up and bring her to the church. We can all leave from there."

"It's perfect, François. But you'll have to hurry—there's not much time left. If we don't leave here by eleven thirty, we won't make it. Our town deserves this!"

"Don't worry, we'll make it."

"To Sainte Marie d'Azur!" cheered Father André.

"To Sainte Marie!" answered the mayor and hung up.

29

The mayor was having a difficult time convincing Bernadette to accompany him to town. He hadn't mentioned the discovery of the lottery ticket because he wasn't certain she didn't share her husband's interest in the ticket. The situation was perplexing him; he'd found her alone at home, but for some reason she was adamantly refusing to go with him. M. François was beginning to lose patience. He knew that every minute lost meant less chance of achieving their goal.

"But Bernadette, it's important for you to come with me. I can't understand why you're resisting. You must realize that if Dominique does something stupid, you'll bear part of the responsibility for not doing anything to avoid it."

"If Dominique does something wrong, he's the only one responsible and he deserves whatever punishment he gets."

"So you're not going to help me?"

"I'm sorry, M. François, but I'm not."

"I hope you're not in agreement with his scheme about the lottery ticket. One village idiot is enough," the mayor ventured, trying to feel Bernadette out about what side she was on.

"Look, Mr. Mayor, it's more than likely this obsession of my husband's is going to cost him his marriage. I don't want anything to do with the lottery. Money isn't everything . . . other things are more important."

From the kitchen Julien heard her words and gave a sigh of happiness.

"All right, Bernadette. I'm going to let you in on a secret that only a couple of people know. The lottery ticket showed up this afternoon at the church. Doubtless one of our citizens felt remorse for all that's happened in the last few months. He wanted his soul to be at peace so he decided to donate it to the church."

"Who was it?"

"We don't know, but the important thing is that we have the ticket. The problem is that Dominique and his friends aren't letting anyone out of Sainte Marie. Now you know today is the last day to redeem the winning ticket. If we don't make it to the notary public's house by midnight, everything that's happened here during the last three months will have been in vain."

Bernadette was silent, not knowing how to respond to this. M. François went on. "The discovery of the ticket was totally unexpected. Besides, there are people from outside the village involved, which could mean worse problems for Dominique. And that's not even taking into account the terrible exposure this means for our village. The people holding the ticket have tried to leave Sainte Marie and have been detained. You're our last hope for our village to return to what it was before. What do you say?"

Bernadette looked at the mayor and behind her at the kitchen, as she'd already done several times. Though M. François had noticed her strange behavior, he hadn't thought anything of it until he heard the creak of a shoe against the wood floor.

"Is there someone else here?" asked the mayor, moving toward the kitchen. Before he reached the door, Julien stepped into the hall.

"Good evening, M. François," said the mailman, his eyes on the floor.

"But . . . what are you doing here, Julien?" the mayor asked in astonishment. The mailman was the last person M. François would have expected to see there. He noticed that Julien's shirt was wet, and not tucked into his pants. The mayor considered Bernadette's strange attitude and put two and two together.

"Look, Mr. Mayor, I—" said Julien.

"You don't owe me any explanations. You're both old enough to do what you like. What I need is an answer from Bernadette. We're running out of time."

"Bernadette, we've got to go with him," said Julien. "Father André has always been kind to us. If it hadn't been for him, today would never have happened. The ticket was found in the church, and it's up to him to administer the offerings made to the saints there. Sainte Marie needs to return to what it was before. You've got to do it!"

Both men waited for Bernadette's answer. Her embarrassment about the situation the mayor had found her in warred with her desire to help Father André. Finally she nodded and said, "All right, I'll do it, but we'll all go together. And not a word about this, Mr. Mayor. We're not ready yet for anyone to know, least of all Dominique."

"Right. Let's go," said M. François. "Let's just hope we make it in time."

The three climbed into the mayor's car. As they drove into the village, Bernadette explained what had happened with Dominique that afternoon and her feelings for Julien, who remained mute in the back seat the whole way. M. François was in complete agreement with Bernadette's course of action. To him, Julien seemed like a good man, unlike Dominique, who had never impressed him, and even less now, with his behavior around the lottery.

M. François parked in front of the church and Julien got out to knock. When the door was opened, Bernadette and the mayor rushed through the pouring rain and entered.

Introductions were made, but what those who had just arrived were really interested in was seeing the famous ticket. Jeanette took it out of her pocket. M. François looked at it, not daring to touch it, while Julien congratulated the priest. Father André looked at Bernadette and said, "It looks as if I should be the one congratulating you."

Bernadette blushed. "It's all happened so fast, Father."

"You don't need to tell me anything now. There will be time to work it all out," he answered. Meanwhile, next to him, Pierre was relating the details of their adventure.

"My children!" interrupted Father André. "There's no time for stories now. It's already eleven fifteen. Let's take both cars."

"I think it's best for the people with most authority from the village to go together," said M. François. "You, Father André, come with me and Bernadette. That will make an impression on them. The rest can go in the other car."

"Very well. Let's go," said the priest. "If things get ugly, I don't want anyone playing the hero. It's only money, after all."

Each followed the mayor's directive and got into their assigned cars. As they drove toward the highway out of town, Father André prayed without stopping while the mayor thought of the glowing terms in which history would describe him after what had happened here tonight. Jeanette thought about how exciting this adventure was and how she would remember it for the rest of her life. Pierre visualized the ways he would expand his bar in order to welcome all the tourists that would throng there to buy lottery tickets. Julien and Bernadette, though temporarily separated in different cars, thought only of each other.

As they neared the intersection with the highway, the sight of Dominique's two friends getting out of their car pulled them out of their private reveries and they all felt a bit nervous about what might happen. "Halt! Access to the highway is prohibited!" Thierry shouted from the middle of the road where he had stationed himself.

In spite of the downpour, everyone piled out of the two cars and went to meet the men barring their way. "We need to pass."

"That's impossible. The highway's closed," said Pamphile.

"Look, my son. We know the highway isn't closed," said Father André. He added, "Say what you will, we're going to proceed."

"You don't know what you're saying, Father," Thierry warned in a threatening tone. "No one's leaving this village until midnight!"

"And who's going to stop us? You?" Pierre puffed up his chest like a prize turkey.

Thierry approached him. "Be careful, you wouldn't want to get hurt."

"That will do," Bernadette said in a no-nonsense voice. "I want to speak to my husband. This has gone far enough."

"Dominique isn't here," said Pamphile, "but if you want, we can call him, I have—"

Thierry cut him off. "We're not calling anyone. If you have anything to say, you can say it to us. I'd like to know why a bunch of townspeople are so interested in getting out of Sainte Marie."

"That's none of your business. We have the right to leave and that's that," answered M. François, taking his cell phone from his pocket and punching in a number. "This is too much. You're not allowing me to leave my own village? I'm calling Chardin right now to come and arrest the two of you."

Thierry snatched the phone out of the mayor's hand and hurled it against the wall of a house, shattering it.

"Have you gone mad?" M. François threw himself at Thierry, who jumped out of his way. The mayor fell to the ground.

A free-for-all ensued. Pierre and Julien shoved Thierry and Pamphile got into the action. In the midst of the confusion, the mayor got to his feet and returned to his car, climbing into the driver's seat and starting the engine. "I'm going to kill this jerk! I'll kill him!" he roared, his window rolled down.

Hearing this, they all stopped and turned toward the mayor's car, which lunged at Thierry. Everyone jumped out of the way except Thierry, who ran for his own car, parked at the curb. He barely had time to get in before M. François's gray 1984 Mercedes sheared off the driver's side door and bashed in his left front fender. The mayor wasn't finished yet, though. He threw the car into reverse for another go, but Thierry quickly started his own engine and backed up a few yards, avoiding a second impact. M. François, on the other hand, was unable to brake in time and crashed head-on into the same wall his phone had shattered against earlier. His hood crumpled and a small column of white smoke began to rise from the engine.

Fearing an explosion, Pierre and Julien ran to rescue the mayor. M. François was conscious but dazed. With the help of the two men, he staggered out of his old Mercedes while Father André contemplated the ruined vehicle and crossed himself.

"He's crazy! He tried to kill Thierry!" exclaimed Pamphile.

"It's your fault for starting this whole mess!" Jeanette rebuked him.

While they were arguing, Thierry had been struggling to turn his car around. Once he had it pointed toward the small group, he shouted at Pamphile, "Get in! I'm going to run them down!"

They all scattered toward Jeanette's car that was parked in the middle of the road. Supported on both sides by Pierre and Julien, M. François hobbled forward as quickly as he could.

"You're insane, this isn't worth it!" yelled Pamphile.

"It's eleven thirty!" Jeanette said to Father André. "We're not going to make it in time!"

Pamphile turned toward Thierry to see if he'd heard too. The other man nodded. Pamphile ran for the car and jumped in just as the rest squeezed into Jeanette's Corolla. As Thierry raced straight toward them, Jeanette cranked the steering wheel and accelerated into a U-turn, careening up onto the sidewalk as Thierry scraped her left rear bumper with his front end.

They fled down the one-way street in the wrong direction toward the center of town. Jeanette fought to maintain control of the car as she plowed through the sheets of water covering the street. Even on high, the windshield wipers did little to aid visibility. When they got to the intersection where Pierre's bar was, Jeanette asked, "Do we turn here?"

"Don't even think about it! With all this water, you'll lose control and we'll crash!" Julien exclaimed. Jeanette continued down the street.

"I thought you didn't know how to drive?" Bernadette said to Julien in surprise.

"I don't, but I love to watch the World Rally Championships and I know all the tricks!" Finally Julien had something he could show off to Bernadette about.

"What do I do? Where are we going?" asked Jeanette, seeing their pursuers close behind.

"Keep going until you get to the government building. The town square's big. You'll be able to turn around without losing speed and still maintain control," Julien told her.

Thierry, guessing Jeanette's plan when he saw her enter the town square, decided to follow her lead. He accelerated until the cars were neck and neck.

"Now we've got them, Thierry!" Pamphile exulted.

Thierry turned the wheel sharply and nudged the Corolla. For an instant, Jeanette thought she'd lost control, but at the last minute she managed to straighten out. When both cars were halfway around the flooded town square, Julien suddenly said, "Floor it and don't move from the center line!"

"Are you sure?" she asked, a little frightened.

"Just do it! I know what I'm saying!"

When Thierry saw Jeanette's car accelerating, he did the same. "We've got them, Pamphile! There's no way out. The ticket is ours!"

"Good work!" Pamphile cheered his friend on nervously.

Meanwhile, in the Corolla, Julien pulled up on the emergency brake and ordered Jeanette, "Put it in first and take your foot off the brake!"

As if to bely Julien's words, the Corolla slowed abruptly. When Thierry saw this, he jammed his foot on the brake as well. The car skidded. What he hadn't realized until that instant was that the final section of the plaza he was driving on was polished granite, whereas the surface beneath the Corolla was brick, with a raised wave-like pattern. Jeanette's car continued to slow little by little on this anti-skid surface, whereas the car containing Thierry and Pamphile slid forward as if on an ice-skating rink. They'd almost reached the end of the town square and were on a direct collision course with the display window of Dominique's bakery. Thierry spun the steering wheel to one side and the other, but his frantic attempts were useless. All the two men had time to do before the car plowed into the display window was cover their terrified faces. The car came to an abrupt halt, wedged inside the bakery. Jeanette drove closer to check on its inhabitants.

"Do you think they're okay?" she asked.

"I'll go see." Pierre got out and approached the wreck.

"I'm sorry, Father," Jeanette said. "It's quarter to twelve—there's no way we can make it in time now."

"Don't worry, daughter. The important thing is that we're all okay," answered Father André, resigned.

"I know how excited you were about how much good this would bring your town. I'm so sorry," insisted Jeanette, a tear trembling on her lower eyelid.

"Just a moment!" exclaimed Julien. "I just thought of something, but I don't know if it will work."

"What?!" asked Jeanette and Father André in unison.

"Hold on." He rolled down the window. "Pierre! Come here!"

"They're unconscious, but otherwise fine. They'll be all right," Pierre said, walking back to the Corolla.

"Pierre, something just occurred to me," said Julien. "Lottery tickets can be redeemed until twelve midnight, right?"

"Yes, of course."

"But if the retailers close at nine, how can you still redeem the tickets until midnight? Where would you go to do it if it was after nine but not yet twelve?"

"What the regulations say is that the national lottery headquarters needs to be informed by midnight that the winning ticket has been presented—for example, by means of a notary public."

"And could the ticket itself be presented at the national headquarters?"

"Well, sure, but that's in Paris, over 430 miles away."

"Obviously I'm not saying we're going to present the ticket there in person, but if there were some way we could prove to them before midnight that we have it, would that work?"

"Yes, but if there's no public official that can attest to it—like a notary—most likely they won't accept it. That way they don't have to pay the prize."

All at once Julien hugged Bernadette and kissed her.

"Have you gone crazy?" she asked, laughing.

"The post office can attest to it! We can send an official fax to the national lottery headquarters before midnight."

"But the post office is closed at this hour," protested Jeanette.

"You're right—but I just happen to be the postmaster of this village, and I have the keys with me!"

"Let's go! We still have time!" Jeanette exclaimed.

"Let's leave the car here. It's nearby, we can walk," put in M. François, newly enthusiastic now that another alternative had been proposed.

They got out of the car and set out for the post office. Passing the bakery, they saw that water from the flooded town square was pouring in through the broken storefront like a waterfall. Bernadette glanced at it and felt nothing.

A Lucky Day

30

August 24

Thierry's voice mail came on again. Dominique had called him four times in the last ten minutes but hadn't been able to get through. This time he left a message. "Would you mind letting me know what the hell you're doing? It's quarter to twelve!" He paused and then added, "Call me!"

Dominique slammed a hand against the steering wheel a couple of times. Next to him, Olivier kept rubbing his own hands, making his growing nervousness clear. The storm was causing him less anxiety than watching his friend's patience wear thin.

"Why don't we drive over to see what they're doing?"

"If they haven't called us, that's supposed to mean everything's fine."

"Maybe they're not answering because something happened. Maybe they had problems with Chardin."

Dominique looked at Olivier fixedly. Maybe he was onto something.

"Have you tried Pamphile? Perhaps he'll pick up," insisted Olivier.

"Of course. I've called both of them. It's really strange.

Maybe it's not such a bad idea to check it out."

"No one's come by here anyway. With this storm, nobody wants to leave home."

"If you have a lottery ticket that's worth 152 million euros to cash in, I don't think you're going to let the weather stop you." Dominique smiled for the first time that night and Olivier felt grateful. *Anything to lighten the mood*, he thought.

"Try once more. If they don't answer, we'll drive over there," he suggested.

As Dominique dialed and put the phone to his ear, he said, "Olivier, I think we've gone about as far as we can with this lottery business."

"Maybe it's for the best," his friend consoled him, patting his shoulder.

"It's possible." As the call rolled to voice mail again, Dominique happened to glance up. "They're not answering again. Let's . . . Wait a minute! Olivier, what's that?"

"Where?"

"There, across the street, on the sidewalk!" Dominique pointed through the windshield at what looked to Olivier like a group of people headed their way.

"It looks like the priest, with Pierre and Julien . . . the mayor, too, and isn't that your wife?"

"What the—"

"There's another woman with them that I don't recognize. I think they're going to the post office." Olivier had never seen Dominique's eyes open so wide.

"Olivier, I told you this Julien knew more than he was

letting on!" exclaimed Dominique.

"What do we do? Your wife's with them."

"This is weird. What do all those people have in common?" Dominique said, wondering what his wife was doing with that group.

Across the street, Julien opened the metal safety door and the main door to the post office and the group filed in, one by one. Bernadette and the mailman were the last ones left on the sidewalk. Thinking they were alone, Julien gave Bernadette a kiss. Across the street, Dominique and Olivier couldn't believe their eyes.

"Dominique, Julien just kissed your wife," Olivier said in a low voice.

"I don't need you to tell me that! I have eyes in my head!" His face congested with wrath, Dominique said, "I'm going to kill that mailman! Let's go!"

He got out of the car and waited under the downpour for Olivier. They crossed the street and went into the post office. Everyone inside froze at the sight of the two men.

"Dominique!" exclaimed Bernadette.

"You shut your mouth. We'll talk at home," snapped her husband.

"Don't treat her like that!" Julien approached Dominique, who knocked him to the floor with a single punch. Bernadette rushed to his side.

"You're insane!" she shouted at Dominique from the floor.

"Why don't we all calm down a little?" put in Father André.

"What are you all doing here?" asked the baker.

"After all this time, the missing ticket appeared in the church," explained Father André. "Now the prize money will be for all of us."

"And who's going to distribute it, you? You've never had enough sense to do anything. The thing to do is to divide it up in equal parts among the people who are here right now," said Dominique.

"The prize money belongs to Father André. It was found in his church, and he's the one who has the right to distribute it among the townspeople according to their need," Pierre said.

"That's absurd. What is a priest going to do with all that money?"

"Whatever he thinks is best! It's none of your business," Julien shot back, getting up.

"You shut your trap or I'll give you more of what I just gave you."

"No. I'm fed up. I've stood it a lot of years, but I'm not going to take it any more."

Dominique waggled his head from side to side in scorn as he sneered, "And just what are you planning to do, you pathetic little wimp of a mailman?"

"The first thing you need to know is that Bernadette and I love each other. She's leaving you."

"Don't talk nonsense." Remembering the kiss he'd seen outside, Dominique turned to his wife and asked, "Is this true, Bernadette?" She remained silent. "I asked you if it's true!" he shouted.

"Yes! It's true. I'm sick and tired of your lies. You've never loved me, and now I know I don't love you either. I love Julien, and I'm going to be with him."

At these words, Dominique lunged at Julien, swinging his fist. The mailman managed to dodge the blow, but Olivier kicked him in the shin. Pierre shoved Olivier into the glass door, shattering it. Meanwhile, Julien got up and delivered a punch with his right fist squarely in the middle of the baker's face. Dominique stepped back, but Julien followed up with his left fist, splitting Dominique's lower lip. A third punch propelled the baker out of the post office and onto the sidewalk outside. On his knees, Dominique begged the mailman not to hit him again. Julien relented and turned his back on the baker. Dominique got up and hit him in the back, knocking him to the ground and kicking him savagely. When he lifted his boot to deliver another kick, Julien grabbed it, throwing Dominique off balance. Quickly springing to his feet, Julien punched him over and over until Dominique began to lose consciousness. At this point Bernadette stepped in, entreating Julien to stop, saying he wasn't worth it.

Julien went back into the post office as Pierre gave Olivier a final shove, depositing him on the sidewalk next to Dominique. "You should go see the state your bakery's in, thanks to your friends." At this, Olivier pulled Dominique to his feet. The two men limped to their car and drove off down the block.

Inside the post office, Julien sank into a chair and Bernadette dabbed at his face with a wet cloth. "He won't be bothering us again," he told her.

"You're my hero! I love you!" she said, dropping kisses on his head. To Julien, each kiss felt like a blow from a cudgel, but he wouldn't have traded that moment for any other he'd lived so far.

"Julien! It's five minutes to twelve. You have to send the fax!" Jeanette interrupted.

The mailman stood up, asked her for the ticket, and went to his workspace. Turning on the computer, he placed the ticket on the scanner and typed,

To National Lottery Headquarters

I, Julien Bélanger Girardon, Postmaster of Post Office No. 1 in Sainte Marie d'Azur, do attest that I did receive, prior to the hour of twelve midnight on August 24th of the current year, the attached lottery ticket with the winning number from the May 24th EuroMillions drawing. I received this ticket from Mr. André Bonmatí Puigvert, parish priest of the Sainte Marie d'Incarnation church, located in this municipal district. The priest has informed me that he desires to redeem this ticket as long as this transaction can be carried out before the final deadline of midnight.

ATTACHMENT: THE WINNING LOTTERY TICKET

Julien fed the ticket into the scanner as everyone watched with bated breath, then clicked on various computer keys. Father André held Jeanette's hand and Pierre perspired copiously.

"It's almost midnight!" M. François broke the tense silence.

"Relax. That's it. It's going through." They all gathered around as Julien smiled.

All at once, the electricity went off. No one laughed this time. There was instant pandemonium as everyone spoke at once. "Silence!" shouted M. François, effectively quieting them all.

Pierre lit a match and peered at Julien through the darkness. "Did the fax go through?"

"I don't know. I pressed *Send*, but I don't know if it went through. There wasn't time to receive the report."

"So now what?" asked M. François.

"Now we wait till the electricity comes back on, check the report, and pray it went through."

Silence fell as the clock in the church tower began to strike midnight. The twelfth stroke died away and was replaced by the steady patter of the rain. No one moved. Father André murmured prayers, Pierre and the mayor stood together in silence, Bernadette stroked Julien's arm, and Jeanette felt her eyes filling with tears. She couldn't believe that after everything they'd been through, after coming so close, they could lose it now.

The seconds crept by. No one could think of anything else; their minds were fixed on what had just happened and everything that had led up to it.

A neon tube blinked a couple of times, anticipating the return of the electricity. The computer booted up and the lights on the scanner winked on. Julien remembered the ticket was still on it. He took it out and handed it to Father André. "Here you are, Father," he said, adding, "Don't lose it! It may be worth a fortune. Who knows?"

"Don't make jokes, my child," answered the priest.

"Well?" asked M. François.

"I don't know yet. I have to see the report." Julien restarted the computer as everyone gathered around, their eyes fixed on the screen. The clock on the wall read 12:04. "Here it comes," said Julien.

The printer began to rattle and a sheet of paper slowly emerged. When the printer went silent again, Julien picked up the report and stared at it for a few seconds while everyone else waited on pins and needles.

"What?!" asked Bernadette.

"*Received at 11:58 p.m. on August 24!*" Julien gave the sheet to Pierre and threw his arms around Bernadette, unable to stop himself.

The report was passed from hand to hand. Everyone hooted and embraced each other. M. François couldn't stop laughing and Pierre tried to pick Father André up, but the priest resisted, so he settled for a group hug with Jeanette. Suddenly remembering that Charlie was waiting for her with Adrien, she decided to go back to the church and share her adventures with them. She told the priest, who immediately said he would accompany her.

When they left the inner office they could see through the window that the rain was beginning to taper off. Within a few minutes it had stopped altogether. They all went outside, still hugging each other and laughing. It had turned out to be a lucky day after all.

31

December 24

Ding, dong, ding . . . ! In spite of the ongoing renovations on the bell tower of the Sainte Marie d'Incarnation church, the bells had never ceased to toll at their appointed hours, and today was no exception.

The last note died away. It was midnight. Time had flown since the lottery ticket had appeared. The townspeople were the same as always; well, with a few changes. After the accident that had destroyed Dominique's bakery, he had been so well compensated by the insurance company that he wondered why it had never occurred to him to orchestrate a similar event before. With the money he received, the baker decided to leave town and open his sugar-hearts factory in Italy. He agreed to a divorce with Bernadette under the condition that she keep the children year-round with the exception of two weeks in the summer; and though two weeks could hardly be considered a lengthy period, the baker still considered it a nuisance to have to look after his children on his own for that amount of time.

Neither Thierry nor Pamphile returned to Sainte Marie once Dominique had left. This was probably motivated as much by Sergeant Chardin's threat that he would lock them up on whatever pretext he could find if he ever saw them in the village again as by Dominique's absence. Olivier, left without friends, began to go out with a divorcee from the village who lost no time in straightening him out, forcing him to work two jobs so he could save as much as possible and they could get married sooner.

Brigitte finished her course in depilation of the pubic area and left Sainte Marie as well, taking a job in a beauty salon in Lyon. To judge by the complaints voiced by several of her customers, her newfound skill left much to be desired. Within a month, though, she fell in love with the owner of the salon, who returned her affections and immediately promoted her to manager. The village gossips spread the rumor that she was pregnant by him, something Father André confidently asserted was unlikely. When people asked him why he didn't believe it, however, he refused to explain himself.

The parish priest was now a well-loved figure all over France. After August 24th, Sainte Marie had again become a magnet for journalists, all of whom wanted to interview the priest, and he'd appeared in newspapers all over the world. Father André had used the prize money to establish a foundation for the needy. He also earmarked part of the money for research on unusual childhood diseases and put Jeanette in charge, since her dream had always been to do pediatric research. Neither did he forget his church, which had sustained so much damage when it was burned during the French revolution. Father André decided to reconstruct it based on the original plans conserved in the archbishop's files. Cautioned that the reconstruction could take so many years he might not live to see it finished, the priest said it didn't matter; it would give him something to occupy his time.

Once the fact that the ticket had been deposited in the

offering box for Saint Jude the Apostle became public knowledge, tourism to the village increased exponentially. Bastian couldn't keep up with the demand for his special sausages and decided to expand his butcher shop and hire employees. He was very satisfied with this arrangement and felt that his new employees worked well overall, though they weren't quite as hygienic as he would have wished. He finally obtained permission from the British Museum to study firsthand the artifacts from the Assyrian Empire not on display to the public. Bastian organized a two-month trip to London, leaving instructions to his staff to fill all Madame Babette's orders at no charge. He felt it was the least he could do after the fright she had suffered during the holdup in his butcher shop. For her part, the widow had recuperated quickly and was thinking about signing up for another retiree trip, especially since Bastian would be out of town for two months.

Pierre was thrilled with the outcome of the whole affair. All year long tourists came to his bar wanting to buy lottery tickets, after which they visited the church and prayed to Saint Jude the Apostle for the same luck. His business thrived to such an extent that he decided to open a bakery next door, since Dominique's no longer existed. Pierre had great luck with the sweets he made, particularly the chocolate Saint Judes with surprise gifts for children inside them.

M. François finally had a reason to feel proud. After word got out about how he'd handled the whole affair, he became quite renowned among local politicians as a consultant. Since he belonged to an independent party, the others decided to elect him president of the local group of municipalities. Even though this was the crowning achievement of his career in politics, what made him the proudest was that he was even more loved by his constituents than he had been before the whole business. Sainte Marie had returned to normalcy, and all its inhabitants were happier than ever.

The National Postal Service had bought Julien an electric golf cart that made delivering the mail much more comfortable. He lived with Bernadette and her children, who adored him. Never did a day go by without him bringing them some sort of present when he arrived home, whatever he'd run across that day—some nuts, a bicycle bell. One day he even brought home a hedgehog that they named Puopi. Julien was happy. He didn't waste time ruing the many years he'd lost with Bernadette but instead tried to take advantage of every minute they had together. They had decided to have a child, and both hoped it would be a girl. They'd even chosen a name: she would be called Chance, which meant "luck" in French.

One day, while Father André was directing the men working on the façade of the church, Julien drove up in his little yellow golf cart. He pulled up next to the priest and got out, holding a small sack of letters.

"Good morning, Father André. How are the renovations coming along?"

"Good morning, Julien. The workers are driving me crazy. They say they're leaving at one o'clock today. At this pace we'll never be finished!"

"They already told you it was going to be a long process. Besides, it's Christmas Eve. The workers need to go home to get ready for their holiday dinners. You're turning into a tyrant!" Julien said, laughing.

"You're right, my son. It's just that I want people to be able to have access to the church by today or tomorrow. We're expecting a full house, something that's never happened in Sainte Marie! I'm nervous about it. Besides, the last thing we need is for there to be some sort of accident."

"Don't worry. Everything will turn out fine. It always

does." As Julien spoke the words, both men thought of the night of the storm. It stood to reason that if things had turned out right that night, anything was possible.

"By the way, Father André," Julien said with interest, "is there any more news about who left the ticket in the church?"

"None at all. It's a complete mystery. We may never know."

"It's just amazing that someone in this day and age would give such an enormous amount. Whoever it was certainly doesn't have to worry about getting into Heaven!"

"You said it!" agreed Father André.

"Well, I'll leave you this sack of letters for the foundation. This is the last thing I had to do and now I'm on my way home. We'll see you tonight at midnight Mass. By the way, would you like to have dinner with us tonight?"

"I'm grateful for the invitation, Julien, but I'm already having dinner with Jeanette and Adrien. They're coming to stay for a few days. The mayor wants to officially proclaim little Charlie an adopted son of Sainte Marie d'Azur."

"Of course. If it hadn't been for them, the ticket wouldn't have been found in time. We'll see you tonight, then."

"Very well. See you later, my son." Father André took the sack of letters and watched as Julien's cart disappeared down the street. He lifted his eyes to the sky. There wasn't a single cloud to mar the blue. Again, the priest wondered briefly who had left the ticket for Saint Jude, then lowered his eyes until they rested on a pair of lounging workers.

"Oh no, here we go again!" he said.

A Lucky Day

32

May 22

"Please form a semicircle around me," the guide directed the group of twenty retired tourists.

The group moved slowly into a rough approximation of a semicircle. Most had cameras hanging around their necks and constantly snapped pictures of the interior of the Sainte Marie church.

"As you can see, little remains of the original church but its bell tower, which dates from the seventeenth century. Though the church is consecrated to Sainte Marie d'Incarnation, its true gem is this image of Saint John the Baptist." There was a volley of camera flashes that temporarily blinded the guide. "It's said that this image, sculpted by an unknown artist, is the oldest in the French Mediterranean area. It was donated by the fifteenth Marquis of Sainte Marie in the middle of the eighteenth century. During the French Revolution, it was buried beneath one of the church courtyards to keep it from being burned, a fate the church itself did not escape. Now if you look up . . ."

"It doesn't seem like such a big deal to me," whispered a

seventy-ish female tourist in a noticeable Canadian accent.

"I thought it was beautiful," answered her husband, also in a whisper. It was obvious from his accent that he hailed from Quebec.

"Darling, what if we look at the church on our own?" his wife suggested.

"Whatever you'd like," he answered. They walked surreptitiously away from the group and turned into a wooden pew to reach the other side of the church. Passing by two confessionals, they saw that one had a green light on above it, something the husband found amusing. "Did you see, dear? The priest's traffic light is green."

Both smiled at this and approached the confessional. Inside sat a priest reading by the light of a small lamp. Seeing that the clergyman was perusing a huge book on Renaissance art, the Canadian tourist wiped the smile off his face and nodded. "Good morning, Father."

The priest gave him a curt nod in reply, causing the Canadian to take several quick steps back until he was out of sight of the clergyman.

They walked down one of the side aisles, passing several icons that held little interest for them. When they'd almost reached the altar, the woman paused before the final image and exclaimed, "St. Jude the Apostle!"

"What a lovely coincidence, don't you think?" said her husband.

"No one will believe it when I tell them about it back at our parish church in Quebec! He has the axe just like ours. There aren't very many left that are holding an axe, you know?" She positioned herself next to the statue and said, "Take a picture of me!"

The Canadian raised his camera and that area of the church, which was quite dark, was momentarily illuminated by the flash. Alarmed, the priest stuck his head out of the confessional. The tourist put her hand into her pocket in search of a couple of coins.

"Can you give me some money? I left my wallet in my jacket on the bus."

"I don't think I have anything on me," her husband replied. "Between the sausages at the butcher shop and the bar, I spent all the cash I had. We'll go to the ATM later."

"What do you mean, you don't have any money left? I gave you ten euros at the bar, and all we had was a soft drink," his wife commented, curious.

"The soft drinks cost four euros," began her husband, seeing that his wife was waiting for an explanation. "Then I saw there were lottery tickets for a drawing day after tomorrow. The grand prize is more than 150 million euros. So I bought one."

"Exactly why would you buy a French lottery ticket if we're going home to Canada next week? Besides, it's probably not even valid since you're a foreigner."

"Of course it's valid," her husband protested.

"Well, we have to leave something for Saint Jude. I don't want any problems with him! Since you don't have any money, you'd better leave him your lottery ticket."

"What do you mean, leave him my lottery ticket?!" he grumbled. Who'd ever heard of giving a lottery ticket to a saint?

"Then you tell me what we can leave him. We have to give something!"

Resigned, her husband opened his wallet and took out the lottery ticket he'd placed inside next to the photo of his two grandchildren. "All right, we'll leave him the ticket, but when we see another lottery retailer I'm going to get another one. It's exciting to play for such an enormous prize—even though there's no chance of winning it."

"Nothing is impossible," said his wife, taking the ticket and depositing it in the metal urn. "If you don't agree, take it up with Saint Jude the Apostle. He's the patron saint of impossible causes."

The raised voice of their guide reached them from the door of the church. "You two, there by the altar, you shouldn't wander off! We're going back to the bus now."

The priest in the confessional stuck his head out again and admonished, "Please, show a little respect! We're in the house of God."

The group of tourists quickly exited the church, leaving undisturbed calm in its wake. Before immersing himself once again in his book on Renaissance art, Father André mused on how noisy the tourists who visited his church always were— but after all, their visits were the only interesting thing that ever happened in the village.

The End

ALSO BY THIS AUTHOR

A Singular
Baptism

CARLOS J. SERVER

Who hasn't had the opportunity, or rather, the trial, of organizing a large family celebration? Thanks to a peculiar family tradition, Lucía, the protagonist of A Singular Baptism, is tasked with arranging the baptism of her son Argimiro on idyllic El Hierro, the smallest of the Canary Islands. During one frantic weekend, Lucía must deal not only with her husband's and her own unconventional families, she must also find out if her suspicions about the true identity of her son's father are correct or merely the result of a simple misunderstanding. With its cast of entertaining characters and everyday situations taken to extremes, A Singular Baptism will leave readers wondering if their families are as outlandish as Lucía's.

Guaranteed fun. A must-read!

ABOUT THE AUTHOR

Carlos J. Server (Valencia, Spain, 1975) first became a household name in 2014 with his debut novel, Un día con suerte, a finalist in the First Annual Indie Literary Prize Contest cosponsored by Amazon, the prestigious Spanish newspaper El Mundo, and publisher Esfera de los Libros. Contest judges considered more than seven hundred works by authors from thirty-two countries. Un día con suerte became an overnight Internet phenomenon, quickly rising in the charts to become the No. 1 bestselling eBook in Spanish on Amazon in Spain, the United States, the United Kingdom, Mexico, Germany, France, Holland, and Italy. It has maintained its ranking in Europe as the top-selling comic novel in eBook form available in Spanish on Amazon throughout 2015 and 2016.

In 2015 Carlos J. Server published his second novel, Un bautizo singular, a romantic comedy of intrigue peopled by a cast of zany characters. The author is currently at work on his third novel, scheduled for publication at the end of 2016.

The global launch of A Lucky Day, the English version of Mr. Server's first novel, took place in February 2017, making the novel available to English-speaking readers everywhere. This will be followed in June of the same year by the publication of A Singular Baptism, the English version of his second novel.

In his fast-paced, suspenseful, highly entertaining novels, Carlos J. Server invites us to enjoy tales reminiscent of Billy Wilder and Woody Allen, two artists much admired by the author.

71637619R00139

Made in the USA
Columbia, SC
01 June 2017